SCRIPTURES FOR
FAITH,
DELIVERANCE,
AND
HEALING

THE TOPICAL SCRIPTURE SERIES

SCRIPTURES FOR FAITH, DELIVERANCE, AND HEALING

JOHN ECKHARDT

CHARISMA
HOUSE

Most CHARISMA HOUSE BOOK GROUP products are available at special quantity discounts for bulk purchase for sales promotions, premiums, fund-raising, and educational needs. For details, write Charisma House Book Group, 600 Rinehart Road, Lake Mary, Florida 32746, or telephone (407) 333-0600.

SCRIPTURES FOR FAITH, DELIVERANCE, AND HEALING
  by John Eckhardt
Published by Charisma House
Charisma Media/Charisma House Book Group
600 Rinehart Road
Lake Mary, Florida 32746
www.charismahouse.com

Cover design by Justin Evans

Visit the author's website at www.johneckhardt.global.

Library of Congress Cataloging-in-Publication Data
Names: Eckhardt, John, 1957- author.
Title: Scriptures for faith, deliverance, and healing / John Eckhardt.
Description: First edition. | Lake Mary, Florida : Charisma House, 2017. |
    Includes bibliographical references and index.
Identifiers: LCCN 2017036751| ISBN 9781629991368 (casebound :
alk. paper) |
    ISBN 9781629991375 (ebook : alk. paper)
Subjects: LCSH: Faith--Biblical teaching. | Spiritual warfare--Biblical
    teaching. | Healing--Biblical teaching.
Classification: LCC BS680.F27 E25 2017 | DDC 234/.131--dc23
LC record available at https://lccn.loc.gov/2017036751

17 18 19 20 21 — 9 8 7 6 5 4 3
Printed in the United States of America

CONTENTS

ACKNOWLEDGMENTS

I WANT TO THANK prophet Lauro Adame for helping me compile and arrange these verses by topic.

Introduction

BY FAITH, HEALING AND DELIVERANCE ARE YOURS

Bless the LORD, O my soul, and forget not all His benefits, who forgives all your iniquities, who heals all your diseases, who redeems your life from the pit, who crowns you with lovingkindness and tender mercies, who satisfies your mouth with good things, so that your youth is renewed like the eagle's. The LORD does righteousness and justice for all who are oppressed. He made known His ways to Moses, His acts to the people of Israel.

—Psalm 103:2–7

HEALING AND DELIVERANCE are two central parts of our salvation experience. It is God's good pleasure to heal you of all your diseases and to set you free from the hand of the enemy. One of the ways we activate these salvation benefits in our lives is through faith in God. Even our small, mustard seed faith can move the mountains of sickness, disease, and demonic oppression from our lives. But there is such a thing as strong faith, and strong faith is built by hearing, and hearing, by the Word of God.

Through the Bible God has given us His word on which we can build a foundation of faith. Psalm 107:20 says, "He sent His word and healed them and delivered them from their destruction." We have access to the healing and delivering power of God every time we open His Word. His Word is alive and active, ready to reveal to us His faithfulness to His people generation after generation. When we read God's Word, we witness the acts of God and His intervention on behalf of His people. We become witnesses to the lovingkindness of God, and our faith is built. We are able to believe that if God did it for them *then*, He will do it for us *now*.

For the past thirty-plus years in ministry healing and deliverance have been my passion. I believe that God wants to see everyone set free and walking in the shalom—peace, prosperity, and blessing—of God. It's what Jesus died for. And if we are tormented by the enemy, we should be able to set up an effective offense and defense against him. It has been my mission to teach and preach the deliverance of God and see His people armed and ready to stand against any devil with the authority of Jesus Christ, who is the living Word of God (John 1:1).

Healing and Deliverance Are Your Covenant Rights

The whole theme of Scripture is about God's covenant with man to rescue, restore, heal, and deliver them, even while they have historically and consistently broken their end of the deal. God remains faithful; man is unfaithful. God keeps covenants; man breaks covenants. But there is always a remnant.

Healing and deliverance come to those who are in covenant with God—the ones who remain faithful. We see an example of this when God told Elijah, "I have preserved seven thousand men in Israel for Myself, all of whose knees have not bowed to Baal and whose mouths have not kissed him" (1 Kings 19:18). These seven thousand men had been faithful to God and to the covenant; they had not worshipped idols. In Scripture they are known as the remnant. We need to understand remnant in terms of covenant. God promised He would save this remnant because of His covenant promises with Abraham, and as the Israelites were part of the seed of Abraham, God extended His covenant of mercy to them. The covenant was simply this, that through Abraham's seed "all the nations of the earth will be blessed." (See Genesis 22:18.)

God made good on His covenant to Abraham by showing His mercy to the people of Israel when they would get into trouble. Because God is righteous, He would judge them, but then His mercy would come, and He would save, deliver, and restore them.

Deliverance out of trouble is a form of God's mercy being enacted because of a covenant. If it weren't for the mercy of God, every covenant violation that we commit today would cause us to be destroyed. Our actions outside of God's plans for our lives put us in violation of the covenant and open us up to all kinds of evil and torment from the enemy. But God has created a way for us to be delivered out of all our troubles, then healed and restored to a place of authority in Him. The Bible says, "Many are the afflictions of the righteous, but the LORD delivers him out of them all" (Ps. 34:19).

It is through Jesus that we now are also the seed of Abraham. We have been grafted in, and because of this covenant we experience the mercy of God. Any work of salvation, healing, and deliverance is an act of mercy on our behalf because of God's covenant with Abraham. When we see God acting on behalf of the people of Israel— delivering them from the hands of their physical enemies, providing for them in the wilderness, and healing them from all their diseases—and then we see Jesus healing all those who were sick and casting out demons from those who were oppressed by the devil, we can see these as acts of God's covenant of mercy.

When Jesus would come into a town, people would say, "Son of David, have mercy on me!" (Mark 10:47; Luke 18:38; see also Mark 10:46, 48–52). They knew that Jesus was in the line of David and David was in the line of Abraham. But this covenant of mercy is much more than forgiveness of sin. Mercy is help for whatever you need help with—healing, deliverance in times of trouble, peace, and prosperity in every area of life. We can therefore imagine that the cry "Son of David, have mercy on me!" could be an expression of any of the following:

- If I need my sins forgiven, have mercy.

- If I need healing in my body, have mercy.

- If I need to be delivered from demons, have mercy.

- If I need breakthrough in finances, have mercy.

God has an infinite amount of compassion and willingness to help and deliver you. His compassion compels Him to want to intervene on your behalf and grant you mercy. And through His covenant you have a right to mercy in the area of healing and deliverance.

Praying and Believing the Word

Many years ago the Lord led me to find key scriptures on healing, deliverance, and warfare and turn them into short prayers. He told me these prayers have power against the enemy when prayed because they are based in the supernatural power of the Word of God. As I began to develop these prayers and declarations and then used them in ministry, we began to see that praying the Word had tremendous power to heal and deliver people from all kinds of bondages. My book *Prayers That Rout Demons* and the others in that series developed out of this season of ministry. To this day we get reports of people being healed and delivered because of these short prayers.

But now the Lord has led me to do something new. He has instructed me to develop topical Bibles on various principles of the kingdom to help people focus in on just what they need from God's Word when they need it. What you have in your hand is a combination of faith, deliverance, and healing scriptures in both the Old Testament and the New Testament: 1) to show you that God is the same yesterday, today, and forever—that if He healed and delivered His people then, He will heal and deliver them today; and 2) to help you develop the discipline to use the power of God's Word to build faith for breakthrough. You do not have to run to your pastor every time the enemy tries to attack you or your family. The Bible is a formidable spiritual weapon that will send devils running out of your life. You have access to one of the most powerful weapons in the spiritual realm. When you speak the Word of God in faith, as Jesus did in the wilderness (Matt. 4:1–11), the enemy will back off. He will have to restore to you sevenfold the things He has stolen.

I encourage you to take these verses and speak them over your situation. There is power in confession. There is power in declaring the benefits of God over every part of your life.

In each section I break down how healing and

deliverance are shadowed and mirrored in each of the testaments. I also break down the Hebrew and Greek meanings of these key words for greater understanding and stronger faith.

I pray that as you read this book, God will bring you to a place of confidence in His desire to save you and to give you an abundant life in the here and now. It is my firm belief that believers do not have to wait until the sweet by and by to experience peace, health, prosperity, and blessing. I believe that the shalom of God is our covenant right for the here and now.

PART I

FAITH
SCRIPTURES

1

LIVING BY FAITH

THE SCRIPTURES REVEAL the importance of faith in the believer's life. Faith is connected to hearing the Word of God. (See Romans 10:17.) And "without faith it is impossible to please God" (Heb. 11:6). We can't even approach God properly without a measure of faith. In 2 Corinthians 5:7 we see that we are called to live by faith and not by sight. Faith is central to the life of a believer, and it affects every area of our lives. In the first part of this book I list every scripture in the Bible concerning faith. This will be an easy reference tool for believers who desire to grow in their faith.

My prayer is that you will be strengthened by these verses. Read them aloud to yourself so you are hearing the Word of God and therefore building yourself up "in your most holy faith" (Jude 20). Unbelief and doubt will hinder you from receiving the promises of God. Fear is another enemy of faith and will hinder you from receiving from the Lord.

1

In the appendix I added some teaching on fasting to overcome unbelief as well as some prayers and declarations to help you build the strong faith you need to see healing and deliverance flow freely in your life.

The following scriptures are key for this section on faith:

> And without faith it is impossible to please God, for he who comes to God must believe that He exists and that He is a rewarder of those who diligently seek Him.
>
> —Hebrews 11:6

> We are bound to thank God always for you, brothers, as it is fitting, because your faith is growing abundantly, and the love of every one of you abounds toward each other.
>
> —2 Thessalonians 1:3

> So then faith comes by hearing, and hearing by the word of God.
>
> —Romans 10:17

2

FAITH IN THE OLD TESTAMENT

IN THE **O**LD **T**ESTAMENT faith is expressed in three ways. The first is the Hebrew word *aman*, meaning agreement or firm regulation; in other words, it is agreeing with God and His Word and saying amen.[1] *Amen* means "to support" or "uphold." It is usually translated "believe."[2] It is used in the context of the kind of faith used when coming to salvation and gives the picture of someone leaning on God (Gen. 15:6). Second, *yaqal* (Job 13:15) means "to trust in extreme pain; to trust under pressure" and is usually translated "hope."[3] The third is *qavah*, the strongest Hebrew word for faith, which is translated as "wait."[4] Psalm 25:5 says, "Lead me in Your truth and teach me, for You are the God of my salvation; on You I *wait* all the day" (emphasis added). Here, "wait" means to "look for, hope, expect; to wait or look eagerly for."[5] Faith and expectancy draw out miracles.

In the Old Testament there are many miraculous stories of people exercising their faith in a God some didn't even know. Their acts of faith were so profound that many of these individuals were mentioned in the "Hall of Faith" found in Hebrews 11. Their stories endured through both testaments, a span that stretched thousands of years. Men and women of God—such as Abel, Enoch, Noah, Abraham, Sarah, Isaac, Jacob, Moses, Pharaoh's daughter, Hannah, Deborah, Ruth, Esther, and many more—are there to help us build faith in the God who leads and guides, and listens and responds.

Genesis

Abram believed the LORD, and He credited it to him as righteousness.

—GENESIS 15:6

Exodus

Then the LORD said to Moses, "Put forth your hand and take it by the tail." And he put forth his hand, and caught it, and it became a rod in his hand. "This is so that they may believe that the LORD, the God of their fathers, the God of Abraham, the God of Isaac, and the God of Jacob, has appeared to you."

The LORD said furthermore to him, "Now put your hand into your bosom." He put his hand into his bosom, and when he took it out, his hand was as leprous as snow.

—EXODUS 4:4–6

If they will not believe you, nor listen to the voice of the first sign, then they may believe the voice of the latter sign.

—Exodus 4:8

But if they will not believe also these two signs or listen to your voice, then you shall take water from the river and pour it on the dry land, and the water which you take out of the river will become blood on the dry land.

—Exodus 4:9

And the people believed. And when they heard that the Lord had visited the children of Israel and that He had looked on their affliction, they bowed down and worshipped.

—Exodus 4:31

The Lord said to Moses, "Indeed, I am going to come to you in a thick cloud, so that the people may hear when I speak with you and always believe in you." Then Moses told the words of the people to the Lord.

—Exodus 19:9

Numbers

The Lord said to Moses, "How long will this people disgrace Me? And how long will they not believe Me, in spite of all the signs which I have done among them?"

—Numbers 14:11

Not so with My servant Moses; he is entrusted with all My house.

—Numbers 12:7

The Lord spoke to Moses and Aaron, "Because you did not believe in Me, to sanctify Me in the eyes of the children of Israel, therefore you will not bring this assembly into the land which I have given them."

—Numbers 20:12

Deuteronomy

Likewise when the Lord sent you from Kadesh Barnea, saying, "Go up and possess the land which I have given you," then you rebelled against the commandment of the Lord your God, and you did not believe Him or listen to His voice.

—Deuteronomy 9:23

He said: I will hide My face from them; I will see what their end will be, for they are a very perverse generation, children in whom there is no loyalty.

—Deuteronomy 32:20

1 Samuel

And I will raise up for Myself a faithful priest; what is in My heart and in My soul he will do it. And I will build him a sure house, and it will walk before My anointed forever.

—1 Samuel 2:35

2 Chronicles

So they rose up early in the morning and went out to the Wilderness of Tekoa. And when they went out, Jehoshaphat stood and said, "Listen to me, Judah and those dwelling in Jerusalem. Believe in the LORD your God, and you will be supported. Believe His prophets, and you will succeed."

—2 Chronicles 20:20

Nehemiah

Over Jerusalem, I put in charge both my brother Hanani and Hananiah, the palace commander, because each was a faithful man and feared God more than many.

—Nehemiah 7:2

…and found his heart faithful before You. And You made a covenant with him to give him the land of the Canaanites, the Hittites, the Amorites, the Perizzites, the Jebusites, and the Girgashites—to give it to his seed. Indeed, You have fulfilled Your words because You are righteous.

—Nehemiah 9:8

Overseeing the replenishing of the storehouse, I appointed Shelemiah the priest, Zadok the scribe, and Pedaiah from the Levites, and to assist them Hanan the son of Zakkur, the son of Mattaniah, for they were considered reliable, and their task was to distribute to their relatives.

—Nehemiah 13:13

Psalms

For there is no uprightness in their mouth; destruction is in their midst; their throat is an open tomb; they flatter with their tongue.

—PSALM 5:9

Help, LORD, for the godly man comes to an end, for the faithful disappear from sons of men.

—PSALM 12:1

Wait on the LORD; be strong, and may your heart be stout; wait on the LORD.

—PSALM 27:14

I believe I will see the goodness of the LORD in the land of the living.

—PSALM 27:13

Oh, love the LORD, all you His saints, for the LORD preserves the faithful, but amply repays the one who acts in pride.

—PSALM 31:23

Rest in the LORD, and wait patiently for Him; do not fret because of those who prosper in their way, because of those who make wicked schemes.

—PSALM 37:7

I waited patiently for the LORD, and He turned to me, and heard my cry.

—PSALM 40:1

Therefore the LORD heard this and was full of wrath; a fire was kindled against Jacob, and anger also came up against Israel, because they did not believe in God nor trust in His deliverance.

—Psalm 78:21–22

The wrath of God came upon them, and He killed the strongest of them and struck down the young men of Israel. For all this they sinned still, and did not believe despite His wondrous works. Therefore He made their days vanish like a breath, and their years in trouble.

—Psalm 78:31–33

My eyes shall be favorable to the faithful in the land, that they may live with me; he who walks in a blameless manner, he shall serve me.

—Psalm 101:6

Then they despised the pleasant land; they did not believe His promise.

—Psalm 106:24

I believed, indeed I have spoken: "I am greatly afflicted."

—Psalm 116:10

Behold, as the eyes of servants look to the hand of their master, and as the eyes of a maiden to the hand of her mistress, so our eyes look upon the Lord our God, until He has mercy upon us.

—Psalm 123:2

Proverbs

A wicked messenger falls into mischief, but a faithful envoy is health.

—PROVERBS 13:17

A faithful witness will not lie, but a false witness will utter lies.

—PROVERBS 14:5

Most men will proclaim everyone his own goodness, but who can find a faithful man?

—PROVERBS 20:6

As the cold of snow in the time of harvest, so is a faithful messenger to those who send him, for he refreshes the soul of his masters.

—PROVERBS 25:13

A faithful man will abound with blessings, but he who makes haste to be rich will not be innocent.

—PROVERBS 28:20

Isaiah

Therefore, thus says the Lord GOD: See, I lay in Zion a stone, a tested stone, a precious cornerstone, firmly placed; he who believes shall not act hastily.

—ISAIAH 28:16

But those who wait upon the LORD shall renew their strength; they shall mount up with wings as eagles, they shall run and not be weary, and they shall walk and not faint.

—ISAIAH 40:31

Who has believed our report? And to whom has the arm of the LORD been revealed?

—ISAIAH 53:1

For since the beginning of the world men have not heard, nor perceived by ear, neither has the eye seen a God besides You, who acts for the one who waits for Him.

—ISAIAH 64:4

Daniel

Then the king was exceeding glad for him and commanded that they take Daniel up out of the den. So Daniel was taken up out of the den, and no manner of harm was found on him, because he believed in his God.

—DANIEL 6:23

Jonah

So the people of Nineveh believed God, and proclaimed a fast. And everyone, great and small, put on sackcloth.

—JONAH 3:5

Habakkuk

Look among the nations, and watch—wonder and be amazed! For I am doing a work in your days that you would not believe, though it were told you.

—HABAKKUK 1:5

For the vision is yet for an appointed time; but it speaks of the end, and does not lie. If it delays, wait for it; it will surely come, it will not delay. Look, his soul is lifted up; it is not upright in him; but the just shall live by his faith.

—HABAKKUK 2:3–4

Look at the proud; his soul is not straight or right within him, but the [rigidly] just and the [uncompromisingly] righteous man shall live by his faith and in his faithfulness.

—HABAKKUK 2:4, AMPC

Look, the one whose desires are not upright will faint from exhaustion, but the person of integrity will live because of his faithfulness.

—HABAKKUK 2:4, NET

3

FAITH IN THE NEW TESTAMENT

IN THE NEW TESTAMENT the word *faith* appears as the Greek word *pistis*, meaning faith, assurance, belief, trust, confidence; fidelity, faithfulness.[1] We find faith in action as part of the miracle ministry of Jesus. Everywhere He went, He healed crowds of people from all their diseases and delivered them from many devils. The people's high level of faith and expectancy caused His healing anointing to flow. Their faith put a demand on Him. In Mark 6:1–6 we are told of a time when Jesus came to His own hometown when there were high levels of unbelief and doubt. The Bible says He could do no mighty work in Nazareth because of their unbelief.

Unbelief blocks healing and deliverance. Faith releases the healing anointing. When you have faith that you will be healed, you draw on the healing power of God. Then His power will be released in your life.

Matthew

Therefore, if God so clothes the grass of the field, which today is here and tomorrow is thrown into the oven, will He not much more clothe you, O you of little faith?

—Matthew 6:30

When Jesus heard it, He was amazed and said to those who followed, "Truly I say to you, I have not found such great faith, no, not in Israel."

—Matthew 8:10

Then Jesus said to the centurion, "Go your way. And as you have believed, so let it be done for you." And his servant was healed that very moment.

—Matthew 8:13

He replied, "Why are you fearful, O you of little faith?" Then He rose and rebuked the winds and the sea. And there was a great calm.

—Matthew 8:26

They brought to Him a man sick with paralysis, lying on a bed. And Jesus, seeing their faith, said to the paralytic, "Son, be of good cheer. Your sins are forgiven you."

—Matthew 9:2

But Jesus turned around, and when He saw her, He said, "Daughter, be of good comfort. Your faith has made you well." And the woman was made well instantly.

—Matthew 9:22

When He entered the house, the blind men came to Him. And Jesus said to them, "Do you believe that I am able to do this?" They said to Him, "Yes, Lord." Then He touched their eyes, saying, "According to your faith, let it be done for you."

—MATTHEW 9:28–29

And He did not do many mighty works there because of their unbelief.

—MATTHEW 13:58

Immediately Jesus reached out His hand and caught him, and said to him, "O you of little faith, why did you doubt?"

—MATTHEW 14:31

Then Jesus answered her, "O woman, great is your faith. Let it be done for you as you desire." And her daughter was healed instantly.

—MATTHEW 15:28

But when Jesus perceived it, , "O you of little faith, why reason among yourselves, that it is because you have brought no bread?"

—MATTHEW 16:8

Then Jesus answered, "O faithless and perverse generation, how long shall I be with you? How long shall I bear with you? Bring him here to Me."

—MATTHEW 17:17

Then the disciples came to Jesus privately and said, "Why could we not cast him out?"

Jesus said to them, "Because of your unbelief.

For truly I say to you, if you have faith as a grain of mustard seed, you will say to this mountain, 'Move from here to there,' and it will move. And nothing will be impossible for you. But this kind does not go out except by prayer and fasting."

—Matthew 17:19–21

But Jesus looked at them and said, "With men this is impossible, but with God all things are possible."

—Matthew 19:26

Jesus answered them, "Truly I say to you, if you have faith and do not doubt, you will not only do what was done to the fig tree, but also, if you say to this mountain, 'Be removed, and be thrown into the sea,' it will be done."

—Matthew 21:21

For John came to you in the way of righteousness, and you did not believe him. But the tax collectors and prostitutes believed him. And even when you saw it, you did not afterward repent and believe him.

—Matthew 21:32

Woe to you, scribes and Pharisees, hypocrites! You tithe mint and dill and cumin, but have neglected the weightier matters of the law: justice and mercy and faith. These you ought to have done without leaving the others undone.

—Matthew 23:23

Who then is a faithful and wise servant, whom his master has made ruler over his household to give them food at the appointed time?

—Matthew 24:45

His master said to him, "Well done, you good and faithful servant. You have been faithful over a few things. I will make you ruler over many things. Enter the joy of your master."

—Matthew 25:21, 23

Mark

When Jesus saw their faith, He said to the paralytic, "Son, your sins are forgiven you."

—Mark 2:5

But He said to them, "Why are you so fearful? How is it that you have no faith?"

—Mark 4:40, nkjv

He said to her, "Daughter, your faith has made you well. Go in peace, and be healed of your affliction."

—Mark 5:34

As soon as Jesus heard the word that was spoken, He said to the ruler of the synagogue, "Do not be afraid, only believe."

—Mark 5:36

And He was amazed because of their unbelief.

—Mark 6:6

He answered, "O faithless generation, how long shall I be with you? How long shall I bear with you? Bring him to Me."

—Mark 9:19

Jesus said, "If you can believe, all things are possible to him who believes."

Immediately the father of the child cried out with tears, "Lord, I believe. Help my unbelief!"

—Mark 9:23–24

Jesus, looking at them, said, "With men it is impossible, but not with God. For with God all things are possible."

—Mark 10:27

Jesus said to him, "Go your way. Your faith has made you well." Immediately he received his sight and followed Jesus on the way.

—Mark 10:52

Jesus answered them, "Have faith in God. For truly I say to you, whoever says to this mountain, 'Be removed and be thrown into the sea,' and does not doubt in his heart, but believes that what he says will come to pass, he will have whatever he says. Therefore I say to you, whatever things you ask when you pray, believe that you will receive them, and you will have them.

—Mark 11:22–24

When they heard that He was alive and had been seen by her, they did not believe it.

—Mark 16:11

He who believes and is baptized will be saved. But he who does not believe will be condemned. These signs will accompany those who believe: In My name they will cast out demons; they will speak with new tongues; they will take up serpents; if they drink any deadly thing, it will not hurt them; they will lay hands on the sick, and they will recover.

—Mark 16:16–18

Afterward He appeared to the eleven as they sat at supper, and He reprimanded them for their unbelief and hardness of heart, because they did not believe those who had seen Him after He had risen.

—Mark 16:14

Luke

And now you will be silent and unable to speak until the day that these things happen, because you did not believe my words, which will be fulfilled in their season.

—Luke 1:20

"For with God nothing will be impossible."

Mary said, "I am the servant of the Lord. May it be unto me according to your word." Then the angel departed from her.

—Luke 1:37–38

Blessed is she who believed, for there will be a completion to those things which were told her by the Lord.

—Luke 1:45

Those along the path are those who hear. Then comes the devil, who takes away the word from their hearts, lest they should believe and be saved. Those on the rock are the ones who, when they hear the word, receive it with joy. But these have no root, for they believe for a while, then in the time of temptation fall away.

—LUKE 8:12–13

When He saw their faith, He said to him, "Man, your sins are forgiven you."

—LUKE 5:20

He said to them, "O fools! And slow of heart to believe what the prophets have spoken!"

—LUKE 24:25

When Jesus heard these words, He marveled at him, and turned and said to the people who followed Him, "I tell you, I have not found such great faith even in Israel."

—LUKE 7:9

He said to the woman, "Your faith has saved you. Go in peace."

—LUKE 7:50

He said to them, "Where is your faith?"

Being afraid, they marveled, saying to each other, "Who then is this Man? He commands even the winds and water, and they obey Him."

—LUKE 8:25

Then He said to her, "Daughter, be of good cheer. Your faith has made you well. Go in peace."

—Luke 8:48

Jesus said, "O faithless and perverse generation, how long shall I be with you and bear with you? Bring your son here."

—Luke 9:41

The apostles said to the Lord, "Increase our faith."

The Lord said, "If you had faith as a grain of mustard seed, you could say to this mulberry tree, 'Be uprooted and be planted in the sea,' and it would obey you."

—Luke 17:5–6

Then He said to him, "Rise, go your way. Your faith has made you well."

—Luke 17:19

I tell you, He will avenge them speedily. Nevertheless, when the Son of Man comes, will He find faith on the earth?

—Luke 18:8

He said, "What is impossible with men is possible with God."

—Luke 18:27

Jesus said to him, "Receive your sight. Your faith has saved you."

—Luke 18:42

He said to him, "Well done, good servant! Because you have been faithful in very little, take authority over ten cities."

—Luke 19:17

But I have prayed for you that your faith may not fail. And when you have repented, strengthen your brothers.

—Luke 22:32

But their words seemed like fables to them, and they did not believe them.

—Luke 24:11

John

Yet to all who received Him, He gave the power to become sons of God, to those who believed in His name.

—John 1:12

If I have told you earthly things and you do not believe, how will you believe if I tell you heavenly things?

—John 3:12

For God so loved the world that He gave His only begotten Son, that whoever believes in Him should not perish, but have eternal life.

—John 3:16

Then Jesus said to him, "Unless you see signs and wonders, you will not believe."

—John 4:48

Jesus said to him, "Go your way. Your son lives."

And the man believed the word that Jesus spoke to him, and he went his way.

—JOHN 4:50

You do not have His word abiding in you, for you do not believe the One He has sent.

—JOHN 5:38

How can you believe, who receive glory from one another and do not seek the glory that comes from the only God?

—JOHN 5:44

Jesus answered them, "This is the work of God, that you believe in Him whom He has sent."

—JOHN 6:29

"But there are some of you who do not believe." For Jesus knew from the beginning who they were who did not believe, and who it was who would betray Him.

—JOHN 6:64

Jesus answered them, "I told you, and you did not believe. The works that I do in My Father's name bear witness of Me."

—JOHN 10:25

Though He had done so many signs before them, yet they did not believe in Him.

—JOHN 12:37

Then He said to Thomas, "Put your finger here, and look at My hands. Put your hand here and place it in My side. Do not be faithless, but believing."

—John 20:27

Jesus said to him, "Thomas, because you have seen Me, you have believed. Blessed are those who have not seen, and have yet believed."

—John 20:29

Acts

And His name, by faith in His name, has made this man strong, whom you see and know. And faith which comes through Him has given him perfect health in your presence.

—Acts 3:16

And what was said pleased the whole multitude, and they chose Stephen, who was a man full of faith and of the Holy Spirit, and Philip, and Procorus, and Nicanor, and Timon, and Parmenas, and Nicolas, a proselyte from Antioch.

—Acts 6:5

So the word of God spread, and the number of the disciples grew rapidly in Jerusalem, and a great number of the priests were obedient to the faith.

—Acts 6:7

Now Stephen, full of faith and power, did great wonders and miracles among the people.

—Acts 6:8

For he was a good man, full of the Holy Spirit and of faith. And many people were added to the Lord.

—Acts 11:24

But Elymas the sorcerer (which is his name by interpretation) opposed them, trying to divert the proconsul from the faith.

—Acts 13:8

Look, you scoffers, marvel and perish! For I will perform a work in your days which you will never believe, even if someone declares it to you.

—Acts 13:41

In Lystra there sat a man, crippled in his feet, who had never walked and was lame from birth. He heard Paul speaking, who looked intently at him and perceived that he had faith to be healed and said with a loud voice, "Stand upright on your feet." And he jumped up and walked.

—Acts 14:8–10

…strengthening the minds of the disciples and exhorting them to continue in the faith, to go through many afflictions and thus enter the kingdom of God.

—Acts 14:22

When they arrived and had assembled the church, they reported what God had done through them and how He had opened the door of faith to the Gentiles.

—Acts 14:27

...and made no distinction between them and us, and purified their hearts by faith.

—Acts 15:9

So the churches were strengthened in the faith, and increased in number daily.

—Acts 16:5

When she and her household were baptized, she entreated us, saying, "If you have judged me to be faithful to the Lord, come to my house and remain there." And she persuaded us.

—Acts 16:15

...testifying to both Jews and Greeks of repentance toward God and of faith in our Lord Jesus Christ.

—Acts 20:21

...to open their eyes and to turn them from darkness to light, and from the power of Satan to God, that they may receive forgiveness of sins and an inheritance among those who are sanctified by faith in Me.

—Acts 26:18

Romans

Through Him we have received grace and apostleship for the obedience of faith among all nations for His name.

—Romans 1:5

First, I thank my God through Jesus Christ for you all, because your faith is spoken of throughout the whole world.

—ROMANS 1:8

This is so that I may be encouraged together with you by each other's faith, both yours and mine.

—ROMANS 1:12

For in it the righteousness of God is revealed from faith to faith. As it is written, "The just shall live by faith."

—ROMANS 1:17

What if some did not believe? Would their unbelief nullify the faithfulness of God?

—ROMANS 3:3

This righteousness of God comes through faith in Jesus Christ to all and upon all who believe, for there is no distinction.

—ROMANS 3:22

…whom God has set forth to be a propitiation through faith, in His blood, for a demonstration of His righteousness, because in His forbearance God had passed over the sins previously committed.

—ROMANS 3:25

Where is boasting then? It is excluded. By what law? Of works? No, but by the law of faith.

—ROMANS 3:27

Therefore we conclude that a man is justified by faith without the works of the law.

—Romans 3:28

It is one God, who shall justify the circumcised by faith, and the uncircumcised through faith.

—Romans 3:30

Do we then make the law void through faith? God forbid! Instead, we establish the law.

—Romans 3:31

But to him who does not work, but believes in Him who justifies the ungodly, his faith is credited as righteousness.

—Romans 4:5

Does this blessedness then come upon the circumcised only, or upon the uncircumcised also? We are saying that faith was credited to Abraham as righteousness.

—Romans 4:9

And he received the sign of circumcision, a seal of the righteousness of the faith that he had while being uncircumcised, so that he might be the father of all those who believe, though they are uncircumcised, that righteousness might be credited to them also.

—Romans 4:11

...and the father of circumcision to those who are not of the circumcision only, but who also walk in the steps of the faith of our father Abraham, which he had while still being uncircumcised.

—ROMANS 4:12

It was not through the law that Abraham and his descendants received the promise that he would be the heir of the world, but through the righteousness of faith. For if those who are of the law become heirs, faith would be made void and the promise nullified.

—ROMANS 4:13–14

Therefore the promise comes through faith, so that it might be by grace, that the promise would be certain to all the descendants, not only to those who are of the law, but also to those who are of the faith of Abraham, who is the father of us all.

—ROMANS 4:16

Against all hope, he believed in hope, that he might become the father of many nations according to what was spoken, "So shall your descendants be." And not being weak in faith, he did not consider his own body to be dead (when he was about a hundred years old), nor yet the deadness of Sarah's womb.

—ROMANS 4:18–19

He did not waver at the promise of God through unbelief, but was strong in faith, giving glory to God.

—ROMANS 4:20

Therefore, since we have been justified by faith, we have peace with God through our Lord Jesus Christ, through whom we also have access by faith into this grace in which we stand, and so we rejoice in hope of the glory of God.

—Romans 5:1–2

What shall we say then? The Gentiles, who did not pursue righteousness, have attained righteousness, even the righteousness which is by faith.

—Romans 9:30

Why not? Because they did not seek it by faith, but by the works of the law. For they stumbled over the stumbling stone.

—Romans 9:32

But what does it say? "The word is near you, in your mouth and in your heart." This is the word of faith that we preach: that if you confess with your mouth Jesus is Lord, and believe in your heart that God has raised Him from the dead, you will be saved.

—Romans 10:8–9

Everyone who calls on the name of the Lord shall be saved.

How then shall they call on Him in whom they have not believed? And how shall they believe in Him of whom they have not heard? And how shall they hear without a preacher? And how shall they preach unless they are sent? As it is written: "How beautiful are the feet of those who preach the gospel of peace, who bring good news of good things!"

—ROMANS 10:13–15

So then faith comes by hearing, and hearing by the word of God.

—ROMANS 10:17

This is correct. They were broken off because of unbelief, but you stand by faith. Do not be arrogant, but fear.

—ROMANS 11:20

For I say, through the grace given to me, to everyone among you, not to think of himself more highly than he ought to think, but to think with sound judgment, according to the measure of faith God has distributed to every man.

—ROMANS 12:3

We have diverse gifts according to the grace that is given to us: if prophecy, according to the proportion of faith.

—ROMANS 12:6

Welcome him who is weak in faith, but not for the purpose of arguing over opinions.

—ROMANS 14:1

The faith that you have, have as your own conviction before God. Happy is he who does not condemn himself in what he approves.

—ROMANS 14:22

But he who doubts is condemned if he eats, because it is not from faith, for whatever is not from faith is sin.

—Romans 14:23

But now is revealed by the prophetic Scriptures according to the commandment of the everlasting God, made known to all the Gentiles for the obedience of faith.

—Romans 16:26

1 Corinthians

God is faithful, and by Him you were called to the fellowship of His Son, Jesus Christ our Lord.

—1 Corinthians 1:9

Your faith should not stand in the wisdom of men, but in the power of God.

—1 Corinthians 2:5

Moreover it is required in stewards that a man be found faithful.

—1 Corinthians 4:2

Therefore I have sent Timothy to you. He is my beloved son and is faithful in the Lord. He will remind you of my ways which are in Christ, as I teach everywhere in every church.

—1 Corinthians 4:17

Now concerning virgins, I have no command from the Lord. Yet I will give my judgment as one who has obtained mercy from the Lord to be faithful.

—1 Corinthians 7:25

No temptation has taken you except what is common to man. God is faithful, and He will not permit you to be tempted above what you can endure, but will with the temptation also make a way to escape, that you may be able to bear it.

—1 Corinthians 10:13

...to another faith by the same Spirit, to another gifts of healings by the same Spirit.

—1 Corinthians 12:9

If I have the gift of prophecy, and understand all mysteries and all knowledge, and if I have all faith, so that I could remove mountains, and have not love, I am nothing.

—1 Corinthians 13:2

So now abide faith, hope, and love, these three. But the greatest of these is love.

—1 Corinthians 13:13

If Christ has not risen, then our preaching is vain, and your faith is also vain.

—1 Corinthians 15:14

If Christ is not raised, your faith is vain; you are still in your sins.

—1 Corinthians 15:17

Watch, stand fast in the faith, be bold like men, and be strong.

—1 Corinthians 16:13

2 Corinthians

For all the promises of God in Him are "Yes," and in Him "Amen," to the glory of God through us.

—2 Corinthians 1:20

Not that we have dominion over your faith, but we are fellow workers for your joy, for by faith you stand.

—2 Corinthians 1:24

We have the same spirit of faith. As it is written, "I believed, and therefore I have spoken." So we also believe and therefore speak.

—2 Corinthians 4:13

For we walk by faith, not by sight.

—2 Corinthians 5:7

But as you abound in everything—in faith, in utterance, in knowledge, in all diligence, and in your love to us—see that you abound in this grace also.

—2 Corinthians 8:7

Examine yourselves, seeing whether you are in the faith; test yourselves. Do you not know that Jesus Christ is in you?—unless indeed you are disqualified.

—2 Corinthians 13:5

Galatians

They had heard only, "He who persecuted us in times past now preaches the faith which he once destroyed."

—GALATIANS 1:23

Yet we know that a man is not justified by the works of the law, but through faith in Jesus Christ. Even we have believed in Christ Jesus, so that we might be justified by faith in Christ, rather than by the works of the law. For by the works of the law no flesh shall be justified.

—GALATIANS 2:16

I have been crucified with Christ. It is no longer I who live, but Christ who lives in me. And the life I now live in the flesh, I live by faith in the Son of God, who loved me and gave Himself for me.

—GALATIANS 2:20

I want to learn only this from you: Did you receive the Spirit through the works of the law, or by hearing with faith?

—GALATIANS 3:2

Does God give you the Spirit and work miracles among you by the works of the law, or by hearing with faith?

—GALATIANS 3:5

Therefore know that those who are of faith are the sons of Abraham.

—GALATIANS 3:7

And the Scripture, foreseeing that God would justify the Gentiles by faith, preached the gospel in advance to Abraham, saying, "In you shall all the nations be blessed."

—Galatians 3:8

So then those who are of faith are blessed with faithful Abraham.

—Galatians 3:9

Now it is evident that no man is justified by the law in the sight of God, for "The just shall live by faith."

—Galatians 3:11

But the law is not of faith, for "The man who does them shall live by them."

—Galatians 3:12

...so that the blessing of Abraham might come on the Gentiles through Jesus Christ, that we might receive the promise of the Spirit through faith.

—Galatians 3:14

But the Scripture has confined all things under sin, that the promise through faith in Jesus Christ might be given to those who believe.

—Galatians 3:22

But before faith came, we were imprisoned under the law, kept for the faith which was later to be revealed.

—Galatians 3:23

So the law was our tutor to bring us to Christ, that we might be justified by faith.

—GALATIANS 3:24

But now that faith has come, we are no longer under a tutor.

—GALATIANS 3:25

You are all sons of God by faith in Christ Jesus.

—GALATIANS 3:26

For we, through the Spirit, by faith, eagerly wait for the hope of righteousness.

—GALATIANS 5:5

For in Christ Jesus neither circumcision nor uncircumcision means anything, but faith which works through love.

—GALATIANS 5:6

But the fruit of the Spirit is love, joy, peace, patience, gentleness, goodness, faith…

—GALATIANS 5:22

Therefore, as we have opportunity, let us do good to all people, especially to those who are of the household of faith.

—GALATIANS 6:10

Ephesians

Therefore I also, after hearing of your faith in the Lord Jesus and your love toward all the saints…

—EPHESIANS 1:15

For by grace you have been saved through faith, and this is not of yourselves. It is the gift of God.

—EPHESIANS 2:8

...in whom we have boldness and confident access through faith in Him.

—EPHESIANS 3:12

...and that Christ may dwell in your hearts through faith; that you, being rooted and grounded in love...

—EPHESIANS 3:17

...one Lord, one faith, one baptism...

—EPHESIANS 4:5

...until we all come into the unity of the faith and of the knowledge of the Son of God, into a complete man, to the measure of the stature of the fullness of Christ...

—EPHESIANS 4:13

...and above all, taking the shield of faith, with which you will be able to extinguish all the fiery arrows of the evil one.

—EPHESIANS 6:16

Philippians

Having this confidence, I know that I shall remain and continue with you all for your joyful advancement of the faith.

—PHILIPPIANS 1:25

Only let your conduct be worthy of the gospel of Christ, that whether or not I come and see you, I may hear of your activities, that you are standing fast in one spirit, with one mind, striving together for the faith of the gospel.

—Philippians 1:27

Yes, and even if I am offered upon the sacrifice and service of your faith, I take delight and rejoice with you all.

—Philippians 2:17

...and be found in Him, not having my own righteousness which is from the law, but that which is through faith in Christ, the righteousness which is of God on the basis of faith...

—Philippians 3:9

Colossians

To the saints and faithful brothers in Christ who are at Colosse:

Grace to you and peace from God our Father and the Lord Jesus Christ.

—Colossians 1:2

For we heard of your faith in Christ Jesus and your love for all the saints.

—Colossians 1:4

And you also learned of Epaphras, our dear fellow servant, who is a faithful minister of Christ for you.

—Colossians 1:7

If you continue in the faith, grounded and settled, and are not removed from the hope of the gospel, which you have heard, and which was preached to every creature which is under heaven, and of which I, Paul, have become a servant.

—Colossians 1:23

For though I am absent in the flesh, yet I am with you in spirit, rejoicing and seeing your orderliness and the steadfastness of your faith in Christ.

—Colossians 2:5

Walk in Him, rooted and built up in Him and established in the faith, as you have been taught, and abounding with thanksgiving.

—Colossians 2:6–7

You were…buried with Him in baptism, in which also you were raised with Him through the faith of the power of God, who has raised Him from the dead.

—Colossians 2:11–12

Tychicus, who is a beloved brother and a faithful minister and fellow servant in the Lord, will tell you all the news about me.

—Colossians 4:7

…with Onesimus, a faithful and beloved brother, who is one of you. They will make known to you everything which is happening here.

—Colossians 4:9

1 Thessalonians

... remembering without ceasing your work of faith, labor of love, and patient hope in our Lord Jesus Christ in the sight of God and our Father.

—1 Thessalonians 1:3

For the word of the Lord sounded out from you not only in Macedonia and Achaia, but also in every place your faith in God has gone forth, so that we do not need to say anything.

—1 Thessalonians 1:8

For this reason we thank God without ceasing because, when you received the word of God, which you heard from us, you received it not as the word of men, but as it truly is, the word of God, which effectively works also in you who believe.

—1 Thessalonians 2:13

We sent Timothy, who is our brother and minister of God and our fellow laborer in the gospel of Christ, to establish and comfort you with regard to your faith.

—1 Thessalonians 3:2

For this reason, when I could no longer endure it, I sent to inquire about your faith, lest by some means the tempter might have tempted you, and our labor might have been in vain.

—1 Thessalonians 3:5

But just now Timothy has come from you to us and brought us good news of your faith and love, and that you always have good memories of us, desiring greatly to see us, as we also desire to see you.

—1 Thessalonians 3:6

Therefore, brothers, during all our afflictions and distress, we have been encouraged about you through your faith.

—1 Thessalonians 3:7

...night and day praying earnestly that we might see your face and might perfect that which is lacking in your faith?

—1 Thessalonians 3:10

But let us, who are of the day, be sober, putting on the breastplate of faith and love, and as a helmet, the hope of salvation.

—1 Thessalonians 5:8

Faithful is He who calls you, who also will do it.

—1 Thessalonians 5:24

2 Thessalonians

We are bound to thank God always for you, brothers, as it is fitting, because your faith is growing abundantly, and the love of every one of you abounds toward each other.

—2 Thessalonians 1:3

So we boast about you in the churches of God for your patience and faith in all your persecutions and tribulations that you are enduring.

—2 Thessalonians 1:4

Therefore we always pray for you that our God would count you worthy of this calling and with power fulfill all your good desires and works done by faith.

—2 Thessalonians 1:11

And pray that we may be delivered from unreasonable and wicked men, for not all men have faith.

—2 Thessalonians 3:2

But the Lord is faithful, who will establish you and guard you from the evil one.

—2 Thessalonians 3:3

1 Timothy

To Timothy, my true son in the faith:

Grace, mercy, and peace, from God our Father and Jesus Christ our Lord.

—1 Timothy 1:2

…nor pay attention to fables and endless genealogies, which cause debates rather than godly edifying, which is in faith.

—1 Timothy 1:4

Now the goal of this command is love from a pure heart, and from a good conscience, and from sincere faith.

—1 Timothy 1:5

I thank Christ Jesus our Lord, who has enabled me, because He counted me faithful and appointed me to the ministry.

—1 Timothy 1:12

The grace of our Lord overflowed with the faith and love which is in Christ Jesus.

—1 Timothy 1:14

...keeping faith and a good conscience, which some have rejected and suffered shipwreck in regard to their faith.

—1 Timothy 1:19

For this I was appointed a preacher and an apostle (I speak the truth in Christ and do not lie), a teacher of the Gentiles in faith and truth.

—1 Timothy 2:7

Yet she will be saved in childbearing if they continue in faith, love, and holiness, with self-control.

—1 Timothy 2:15

...keeping the mystery of the faith in a pure conscience.

—1 Timothy 3:9

For those who have served well in the office of deacon purchase for themselves good standing and great boldness in the faith, which is in Christ Jesus.

—1 Timothy 3:13

Now the Spirit clearly says that in the last times some will depart from the faith and pay attention to seducing spirits and doctrines of devils.

—1 Timothy 4:1

If you remind the brothers of these things, you will be a good minister of Jesus Christ, nourished by the words of faith and of good doctrine, which you have followed closely.

—1 TIMOTHY 4:6

Let no one despise your youth, but be an example to the believers in speech, in conduct, in love, in spirit, in faith, and in purity.

—1 TIMOTHY 4:12

But if any do not care for their own, and especially for those of their own house, they have denied the faith and are worse than unbelievers.

—1 TIMOTHY 5:8

…bring judgment on themselves, because they have cast off their first pledge.

—1 TIMOTHY 5:12

For the love of money is the root of all evil. While coveting after money, some have strayed from the faith and pierced themselves through with many sorrows.

—1 TIMOTHY 6:10

But you, O man of God, escape these things, and follow after righteousness, godliness, faith, love, patience, and gentleness.

—1 TIMOTHY 6:11

Fight the good fight of faith. Lay hold on eternal life, to which you are called and have professed a good profession before many witnesses.

—1 TIMOTHY 6:12

By professing it, some have erred concerning the faith.

Grace be with you. Amen.

—1 Timothy 6:21

2 Timothy

…remembering the genuine faith that first lived in your grandmother Lois and your mother Eunice and that I am persuaded lives in you also.

—2 Timothy 1:5

Follow the pattern of sound teaching which you have heard from me in the faith and love that is in Christ Jesus.

—2 Timothy 1:13

Share the things that you have heard from me in the presence of many witnesses with faithful men who will be able to teach others also.

—2 Timothy 2:2

If we are faithless, He remains faithful; He cannot deny Himself.

—2 Timothy 2:13

…who have erred concerning the truth, saying that the resurrection has already occurred, and who overthrow the faith of some.

—2 Timothy 2:18

So flee youthful desires and pursue righteousness, faith, love, and peace, with those who call on the Lord out of a pure heart.

—2 Timothy 2:22

Now as Jannes and Jambres resisted Moses, so these also resist the truth, men of corrupt minds and worthless concerning the faith.

—2 Timothy 3:8

But you have observed my doctrine, manner of life, purpose, faith, tolerance, love, patience...

—2 Timothy 3:10

Since childhood you have known the Holy Scriptures, which are able to make you wise unto salvation through the faith that is in Christ Jesus.

—2 Timothy 3:15

Titus

Paul, a servant of God and an apostle of Jesus Christ, according to the faith of God's elect and the knowledge of the truth which leads to godliness...

—Titus 1:1

To Titus, my own son in the common faith: Grace, mercy, and peace, from God the Father and the Lord Jesus Christ our Savior.

—Titus 1:4

...holding firmly the trustworthy word that is in accordance with the teaching, that he may be able both to exhort with sound doctrine and to convince those who oppose it.

—Titus 1:9

This witness is true. So rebuke them sharply that they may be sound in the faith.

—Titus 1:13

Older men should be sober, serious, temperate, sound in faith, in love, in patience.

—Titus 2:2

Philemon

Whenever I hear of your love and faith, which you have toward the Lord Jesus and for all the saints...

—Philemon 1:5

...that the sharing of your faith may be most effective by the acknowledgment of every good thing which is in you from Christ Jesus.

—Philemon 1:6

Hebrews

Be attentive, brothers, lest there be in any of you an evil, unbelieving heart, and you depart from the living God.

—Hebrews 3:12

So we see that they could not enter because of unbelief.

—Hebrews 3:19

For the gospel was preached to us as well as to them. But the word preached did not benefit them, because it was not mixed with faith in those who heard it. For we who have believed have entered this rest, as He has said...

—Hebrews 4:2–3

Let us labor therefore to enter that rest, lest anyone fall by the same pattern of unbelief.

—Hebrews 4:11

...so that you may not be lazy, but imitators of those who through faith and patience inherit the promises.

—Hebrews 6:12

Let us draw near with a true heart in full assurance of faith, having our hearts sprinkled to cleanse them from an evil conscience, and our bodies washed with pure water.

—Hebrews 10:22

Now the just shall live by faith; but if anyone draws back, My soul shall have no pleasure in him. But we are not of those who draw back to destruction, but of those who have faith to the saving of the soul.

—Hebrews 10:38–39

Now faith is the substance of things hoped for, the evidence of things not seen.

—Hebrews 11:1

By faith we understand that the universe was framed by the word of God, so that things that are seen were not made out of things which are visible.

—Hebrews 11:3

By faith Abel offered to God a more excellent sacrifice than Cain offered. Through this he was approved as righteous, with God testifying concerning his gifts. He still speaks through his faith, though he is dead.

—Hebrews 11:4

By faith Enoch was taken to heaven so that he would not see death. He was not found, because God took him away. For before he was taken, he had this commendation, that he pleased God.

—Hebrews 11:5

And without faith it is impossible to please God, for he who comes to God must believe that He exists and that He is a rewarder of those who diligently seek Him.

—Hebrews 11:6

By faith Noah, being divinely warned about things not yet seen, moved with godly fear, prepared an ark to save his family, by which he condemned the world and became an heir of the righteousness that comes by faith.

—Hebrews 11:7

By faith Abraham obeyed when he was called to go out into a place which he would later receive as an inheritance. He went out not knowing where he was going.

—Hebrews 11:8

By faith he dwelt in the promised land, as in a foreign land, dwelling in tents with Isaac and Jacob, the heirs of the same promise.

—Hebrews 11:9

By faith Sarah herself also received the ability to conceive seed, and she bore a child when she was past the age, because she judged Him faithful who had promised.

—Hebrews 11:11

These all died in faith not having received the promises, but having seen them from afar were assured of them, embraced them, and confessed that they were strangers and pilgrims on the earth.

—Hebrews 11:13

By faith Abraham, when he was tested, offered up Isaac, and he who had received the promises offered up his only begotten son.

—Hebrews 11:17

By faith Isaac blessed Jacob and Esau concerning things to come.

—Hebrews 11:20

By faith Jacob, when he was dying, blessed each of the sons of Joseph and worshipped while leaning on the top of his staff.

—Hebrews 11:21

By faith Joseph, when he was dying, mentioned the exodus of the children of Israel and gave instructions concerning his bones.

—Hebrews 11:22

By faith Moses, when he was born, was hidden by his parents for three months, because they saw he was a beautiful child, and they were not afraid of the king's command.

—Hebrews 11:23

By faith Moses, when he became of age, refused to be called the son of Pharaoh's daughter.

—Hebrews 11:24

By faith he forsook Egypt, not fearing the wrath of the king. He endured by looking to Him who is invisible.

—Hebrews 11:27

By faith he kept the Passover and the sprinkling of blood, lest the one who destroys the firstborn touch them.

—Hebrews 11:28

By faith they passed through the Red Sea as on dry land, which the Egyptians attempted to do, but were drowned.

—Hebrews 11:29

By faith the walls of Jericho fell down after they were encircled for seven days.

—Hebrews 11:30

By faith the prostitute Rahab, when she received the spies with peace, did not perish with those who did not believe.

—Hebrews 11:31

Time would fail me to tell of Gideon, Barak, Samson, Jephthah, of David and Samuel and the prophets, who through faith subdued kingdoms, administered justice, obtained promises, stopped the mouths of lions...

—Hebrews 11:32–33

These all have obtained a good report through faith, but they did not receive the promise.

—Hebrews 11:39

Let us look to Jesus, the author and finisher of our faith, who for the joy that was set before Him endured the cross, despising the shame, and is seated at the right hand of the throne of God.

—Hebrews 12:2

Remember those who rule over you, who have proclaimed to you the word of God. Follow their faith, considering the results it has produced in their lives.

—Hebrews 13:7

James

The trying of your faith develops patience.

—James 1:3

But let him ask in faith, without wavering. For he who wavers is like a wave of the sea, driven and tossed with the wind.

—James 1:6

My brothers, have faith in our Lord Jesus Christ, the Lord of glory, without partiality.

—JAMES 2:1

Listen, my beloved brothers. Has God not chosen the poor of this world to be rich in faith and heirs of the kingdom which He has promised to those who love Him?

—JAMES 2:5

What does it profit, my brothers, if a man says he has faith but has no works? Can faith save him?

—JAMES 2:14

So faith by itself, if it has no works, is dead.

—JAMES 2:17

But a man may say, "You have faith and I have works." Show me your faith without your works, and I will show you my faith by my works.

—JAMES 2:18

But do you want to be shown, O foolish man, that faith without works is dead?

—JAMES 2:20

Do you see how faith worked with his works, and by works faith was made perfect? The Scripture was fulfilled which says, "Abraham believed God, and it was reckoned to him as righteousness," and he was called the friend of God. You see then how by works a man is justified, and not by faith only.

—JAMES 2:22–24

As the body without the spirit is dead, so faith without works is dead.

—James 2:26

And the prayer of faith will save the sick, and the Lord will raise him up. And if he has committed any sins, he will be forgiven.

—James 5:15

1 Peter

...who are protected by the power of God through faith for a salvation ready to be revealed in the last time.

—1 Peter 1:5

In order that the genuineness of your faith, which is more precious than gold that perishes, though it is tried by fire, may be found to result in praise, glory, and honor at the revelation of Jesus Christ...

—1 Peter 1:7

...receiving as the result of your faith the salvation of your souls.

—1 Peter 1:9

Through Him you believe in God who raised Him up from the dead and gave Him glory, so that your faith and hope might be in God.

—1 Peter 1:21

So then, let those who suffer according to the will of God entrust their souls to a faithful Creator, while continuing to do good.

—1 Peter 4:19

Resist him firmly in the faith, knowing that the same afflictions are experienced by your brotherhood throughout the world.

—1 Peter 5:9

2 Peter

Simon Peter, a servant and apostle of Jesus Christ, To those who have received a faith as precious as ours through the righteousness of our God and Savior Jesus Christ.

—2 Peter 1:1

For this reason make every effort to add virtue to your faith; and to your virtue, knowledge.

—2 Peter 1:5

1 John

For whoever is born of God overcomes the world, and the victory that overcomes the world is our faith. Who is it that overcomes the world, but the one who believes that Jesus is the Son of God?

—1 John 5:4–5

Jude

Beloved, while I diligently tried to write to you of the salvation we have in common, I found it necessary to write and appeal to you to contend for the faith which was once delivered to the saints.

—Jude 3

But you, beloved, build yourselves up in your most holy faith. Pray in the Holy Spirit.

—JUDE 20

Revelation

I know your works, love, service, faith, and your patience, and that your last works are more than the first.

—REVELATION 2:19

"He who is to be taken captive, into captivity he shall go; he who kills with the sword, with the sword he must be killed." Here is a call for the patience and the faith of the saints.

—REVELATION 13:10

Here is the patience of the saints; here are those who keep the commandments of God and the faith of Jesus.

—REVELATION 14:12

These will wage war with the Lamb, but the Lamb will overcome them, for He is Lord of lords and King of kings. Those who are with Him are called and chosen and faithful.

—REVELATION 17:14

PART II

DELIVERANCE
SCRIPTURES

4

DELIVERANCE IS A
GIFT FROM GOD

DELIVERANCE IS A GIFT from God and part of the blessing of being in covenant with Him. It destroys only what is of the devil; it never destroys what is of the Holy Spirit. Since deliverance is a work of the Holy Spirit, it builds up the saints and edifies the church. It tears down the strongholds of the enemy but builds up the work of God.

I wholeheartedly believe in deliverance ministry. I have seen many miracles and thousands of people set free around the world. Every time I do, I thank God for His grace and mercy. I am still learning things in deliverance, and I am believing to see more miracles in the years to come.

Deliverance in the Word

There are numerous scriptures on deliverance. The large number shows us the importance deliverance is given in the Word of God. The following Greek and Hebrew words are part of the lexicon of the ministry of deliverance.

LEXICON OF THE MINISTRY OF DELIVERANCE		
English	**Hebrew**	**Greek**
Binding	*Ecar*—"bond, binding obligation; vow"[1] (Num. 30:2)	*Deo*—to legally bind, binding, or bound (Matt. 18:18); to prohibit, to declare unlawful with imposing a legal ban or prohibition; also, used in prayer, intercession, or spiritual warfare[2] (Matt. 12:29) *Desmeuo*—to bind a heavy legal burden upon one without assistance; to put one in a prison with heavy chains[3] (Matt. 23:4; Acts 22:4) *Desmeo*—to bind, tie, or shackle, as with chains[4] (Luke 8:29)
Cast out, drive out, expel, eject	*Garash*—"drive out, cast out, thrust out, drive away, put away, divorced, driven, expel, drive forth"[5] (Gen. 4:14; Gen. 21:10; 1 Sam. 26:19; 1 Chron. 17:21)	*Ekballo*—to cast out demons[6] (Mark 16:17; Mark 1:34; Luke 4:41)

English	Hebrew	Greek
Deliver	*Natsal* (Ps. 22:8; 25:20)—to take away or snatch away, as to take away riches and wealth (2 Chron. 20:25); to spoil (Exod. 3:22); preserve and defend (Exod. 14:14); to escape as a slave would and to find refuge where there is no extradition (Deut. 23:15–16)[7] *Chalats* (Prov. 11:8)—to be delivered or pulled out as from trouble and death; to withdraw or pull out of [8]	*Rhyomai*—"to draw to one's self, to rescue, to deliver; the deliverer" [9] (Matt. 6:13; Rom. 7:24; Col. 1:13)
Deliverer	*Palat* (Ps. 40:17)—"to slip away; to escape." [10] It describes the One who makes us smooth and slippery by His anointing to escape; the Lord our great deliverer (Ps. 18:2).	*Lytrotes*—"redeemer, deliverer, liberator" [11] (Acts 7:35) *Rhyomai*—the deliverer, refers to Christ [12] (Rom. 11:26); see also "deliver"
Devilish, demonic, diabolical	No Hebrew equivalent found	*Daimoniodes* (James 3:15)—"resembling or proceeding from an evil spirit, demon-like" [13]

English	Hebrew	Greek
Dominion	*Radah*—"to rule, have dominion, tread down; subjugate"[14] (Gen. 1:26–28; Judg. 5:13) *Mashal*—to rule or reign; to have dominion, to exercise power[15] (Ps. 8:6)	*Kyrieuo*—"to be lord of, to rule, have dominion over; to exercise influence upon, to have power over"[16] (Rom. 6:9, 14)
Door	*Pethach*—opening, doorway, entrance, a door to let the captives out of prison[17] (Ps. 24:7; Isa. 14:17)	*Thyra*—door, gate, "the name of him who brings salvation to those who follow his guidance"[18] (John 10:7, 9; Rev. 3:17–20)
Liberty, freedom	*Derowr*—"a flowing, free run, liberty"[19] (Isa. 61:1)	*Aphesis*—"release from bondage or imprisonment; forgiveness or pardon, of sins"[20] And it was Jesus Christ Himself that radiated with the glory of His Father to set the captives free and bring liberty to the bruised (Luke 4:18; John 1:4–5, 14). This is what Jesus meant and wanted His followers to do, to shine with the light of His glory among the people in order to bring liberty to them and glory to the Father (Matt. 5:14–16).

English	Hebrew	Greek
Loosing	*Pathach*—"to open; to be opened, be let loose, be thrown open; to free; to loosen"[21] (Ps. 102:20)	*Lyo*—to unloose, loose; to declare unlawful, allowable; to annul; to abrogate; to legally bring to an end that which was prohibited (Matt. 16:19; 18:18); also to grant freedom; to discharge; to liberate; to undo the heavy chains or to break away; to set free.[22] It makes the powers of sin, sickness, and Satan null and void (Luke 13:15–16).
Oppressed	*Ashaq*—"to press upon, oppress, violate, defraud, do violence, get deceitfully, wrong, extort"[23] (Deut. 28:29)	*Katadynasteuo*—"to exercise harsh control over one, to use one's power against one"[24] (Acts 10:38)
Possessed	No Hebrew equivalent found	*Daimonizomai*—"to be under the power of a demon," or demonized[25] (Mark 1:32)
Satan, devil	*Satan*—accuser, opponent, enemy, adversary, hater, slanderer (Zech. 3:2)[26]	*Diabolos*—an adversary that throws fiery missiles (Matt. 4:1; Eph. 6:16); an enemy, persecutor, murderer, slanderer, critic, and liar[27] (John 10:10)

English	Hebrew	Greek
Savior, salvation; also, deliverance, freedom, healing	*Yasha*—to have ample room enough to shelter and supplies enough for support after being delivered from danger.[28] *Yasha* is used more than one hundred times in the Old Testament, including in Ps. 34:6; Isa. 12:2; 49:26; 52:12–13.	*Sozo*—"to save, keep safe and sound, to rescue from danger or destruction; to save a suffering one (from perishing), heal, restore to health; to preserve one who is in danger of destruction, to save or rescue"[29] (Matt. 18:11)
Vexed	*Ra'a*—"to be bad, be evil; to be injurious; to be wicked; to break; to be broken"[30] (Num. 20:15) *Dachaq*—"to thrust, oppress, crowd"[31] (Judg. 2:18; Joel 2:8)	*Ochleo*—"to excite a mob against one; to disturb; to trouble, molest; to be troubled: by demons"[32] (Luke 6:18) *Kataponeo*—to wear down, "to tire down with toil, exhaust with labour; [hence,] to afflict or oppress with evils; to make trouble for; to treat roughly"[33] (2 Pet. 2:7)

How God anointed Jesus of Nazareth with the Holy Spirit and with power, who went about doing good and healing all who were oppressed by the devil, for God was with Him.

—Acts 10:38

Drive the Enemy Out Through Deliverance

Israel was told to drive out the nations from Canaan and possess the land. This was a type of Christ's ministry in driving out demons, which He commissioned His disciples to do as well. A lack of deliverance will allow the enemy to operate in the lives of believers without interference.

Deliverance is the children's bread (Matt. 15:26). Believers should receive deliverance and minister deliverance.

Common spirits people need deliverance from include:

- Addiction
- Anger
- Bitterness
- Confusion
- Depression
- Discouragement
- Fear
- Guilt
- Hurt
- Infirmity
- Loneliness
- Lust
- Mind control
- Poverty
- Pride
- Rebellion
- Rejection
- Sadness
- Shame
- Unforgiveness
- Witchcraft

Areas of demonization can include the mind, emotions, will, appetite, body, and sexual character. Demons can dwell in different areas of the body, including the stomach, chest, back, head, eyes, glands, shoulders, and even organs. Demons often come out of the air passages in the body.

The word for *spirit* is the Greek word *pneuma*, which means breath, wind, or air.

In this section we are going to connect with all the verses that lead us to deliverance from the enemy and all forms of oppression.

5

DELIVERANCE IN THE OLD TESTAMENT

ELIVERANCE IN THE OLD TESTAMENT mostly manifests in God's delivering the Israelites from their physical enemies. Through wars and battles, we see the Israelites taking occupancy of the land God promised to them. Many times they were small in number, discouraged, or beaten down, but God always let them know that the battle was not theirs; it was His. He sent His angels ahead of them and delivered their enemies into their hands.

In Psalms we get to see a more intimate portrait of deliverance through one of God's chosen, David, who eventually became king of Israel. David doesn't hold back his groaning and crying out to the Lord. David is a picture to us of what it looks like to be in desperate need of deliverance. David was called "a man after God's own heart." He demonstrated what it means to know where your help comes from. Through David's life we come to learn that one of the keys to deliverance is worship. Even while making grave mistakes, David never acted as if he didn't know God was his source and supreme authority.

The Old Testament shows what physical deliverance looks like. It provides a foreshadowing of the spiritual deliverance from our spiritual enemies we now experience as part of the new covenant in Christ.

Genesis

> Then Melchizedek king of Salem brought out bread and wine. He was the priest of God Most High. And he blessed him and said, "Blessed be Abram by God Most High, Creator of heaven and earth; and blessed be God Most High, who has delivered your enemies into your hand."
>
> —Genesis 14:18–20

> When the morning dawned, the angels urged Lot, saying, "Arise, take your wife and your two daughters who are here. Otherwise you will be consumed in the punishment of the city."
>
> —Genesis 19:15

> So it was that when God destroyed the cities of the valley, God remembered Abraham, and sent Lot out of the middle of the destruction, when He overthrew the cities in which Lot lived.
>
> —Genesis 19:29

> Deliver me, I pray, from the hand of my brother, from the hand of Esau. For I fear him, that he

will come and attack me and the mothers with the children.

—GENESIS 32:11

But when Reuben heard it, he rescued him out of their hands, saying, "Let us not kill him."

—GENESIS 37:21

God sent me ahead of you to preserve you as a remnant on the earth and to save your lives by a great deliverance.

—GENESIS 45:7

Judah, your brothers shall praise you; your hand shall be on the neck of your enemies; your father's sons will bow down before you.

—GENESIS 49:8

Joseph said to his brothers, "I am about to die. God will surely come to you and bring you out of this land to the land of which He swore to Abraham, to Isaac, and to Jacob."

—GENESIS 50:24

Exodus

…and they made their lives bitter with hard service—in mortar and in brick, and in all manner of service in the field, all their service in which they made them serve was with rigor.

—EXODUS 1:14

In the passing of time the king of Egypt died. And the children of Israel sighed because of the bondage, and they cried out, and their cry came up to God on account of the bondage.

—Exodus 2:23

Therefore, I have come down to deliver them out of the hand of the Egyptians, and to bring them up out of that land to a good and spacious land, to a land flowing with milk and honey, to the place of the Canaanites, the Hittites, the Amorites, the Perizzites, the Hivites, and the Jebusites.

—Exodus 3:8

Therefore, I said, I will bring you up out of the affliction of Egypt to the land of the Canaanites, the Hittites, the Amorites, the Perizzites, the Hivites, and the Jebusites, to a land flowing with milk and honey.

—Exodus 3:17

I have also heard the groaning of the children of Israel, whom the Egyptians keep in bondage, and I have remembered My covenant. "Therefore say to the children of Israel: 'I am the LORD, and I will bring you out from under the burdens of the Egyptians, and I will rid you out of their bondage, and I will redeem you with a stretched-out arm and with great judgments. And I will take you to Me for a people, and I will be to you a God. And you shall know that I am the LORD your God, who brings you out from under the burdens of the Egyptians.'"

—Exodus 6:5–7

I will put a division between My people and your people. Tomorrow this sign will happen.

—Exodus 8:23

You shall take a bunch of hyssop, and dip it in the blood that is in the basin, and apply the lintel and the two side posts with the blood that is in the basin, and none of you shall go out from the door of his house until the morning. For the Lord will pass through to kill the Egyptians. And when He sees the blood upon the lintel and on the two side posts, the Lord will pass over the door and will not permit the destroyer to come to your houses to kill *you*.

—Exodus 12:22–23

…that you shall say, "It is the sacrifice of the Lord's Passover, who passed over the houses of the children of Israel in Egypt, when He smote the Egyptians, and delivered our households." And the people bowed down and worshipped.

—Exodus 12:27

The Lord shall fight for you, while you hold your peace.

—Exodus 14:14

And as for you, lift up your rod, and stretch out your hand over the sea, and divide it; then the children of Israel shall go on dry ground through the midst of the sea.

—Exodus 14:16

Then Moses stretched out his hand over the sea, and the LORD caused the sea to go back by a strong east wind all that night, and made the sea dry land, so that the waters were divided. The children of Israel went into the midst of the sea on the dry ground, and the waters were a wall unto them on their right hand, and on their left. Then the Egyptians pursued and went in after them into the midst of the sea, even all Pharaoh's horses, his chariots, and his horsemen.

—Exodus 14:21–23

Then the LORD said to Moses, "Stretch out your hand over the sea, so that the waters may come back upon the Egyptians, upon their chariots, and their horsemen."

—Exodus 14:26

Then Moses and the children of Israel sang this song to the LORD and spoke, saying: "I will sing to the LORD, for He has triumphed gloriously! He has thrown the horse and his rider into the sea!"

—Exodus 15:1

Pharaoh's chariots and his army He has thrown into the sea; his chosen captains also are drowned in the Red Sea.

—Exodus 15:4

Miriam answered them, "Sing to the LORD, for He triumphed gloriously! The horse and his rider He has hurled into the sea."

—Exodus 15:21

Jethro rejoiced because of all the goodness which the LORD had done for Israel, whom He had delivered out of the hand of the Egyptians.

—EXODUS 18:9

Jethro said, "The LORD be blessed, who has delivered you out of the hand of the Egyptians, and out of the hand of Pharaoh, who has delivered the people from under the hand of the Egyptians."

—EXODUS 18:10

You must not allow a sorceress to live.

—EXODUS 22:18

I will send hornets before you which shall drive out the Hivite, the Canaanite, and the Hittite from before you.

—EXODUS 23:28

I will not drive them out before you in one year, lest the land become desolate and the beasts of the field multiply against you.

—EXODUS 23:29

Little by little I will drive them out before you, until you become fruitful and inherit the land.

—EXODUS 23:30

For I will drive out the nations before you and enlarge your borders. No man will covet your land when you go up to appear before the LORD your God three times in the year.

—EXODUS 34:24

Leviticus

For I am the Lord who brings you up out of the land of Egypt to be your God. Therefore you shall be holy, for I am holy.

—Leviticus 11:45

They shall no more offer their sacrifices to goat demons, after whom they have acted like whores. This shall be a perpetual statute for them throughout their generations.

—Leviticus 17:7

Do not defile yourselves in any of these ways, for in these practices the nations I am casting out before you have defiled themselves.

—Leviticus 18:24

You shall not walk in the customs of the nation that I am driving out before you, for they committed all these things, and therefore I abhorred them.

—Leviticus 20:23

You shall consecrate the fiftieth year, and proclaim liberty throughout all the land to all the inhabitants. It shall be a Jubilee to you, and each of you shall return to his possession, and every person shall return to his family.

—Leviticus 25:10

You shall chase your enemies, and they shall fall before you by the sword.

—Leviticus 26:7

Five of you shall chase a hundred, and a hundred of you shall put ten thousand to flight, and your enemies shall fall before you by the sword.

—LEVITICUS 26:8

Numbers

The LORD listened to the voice of Israel and delivered up the Canaanites, and they utterly destroyed them and their cities, and he called the name of the place Hormah.

—NUMBERS 21:3

Then you will drive out all the inhabitants of the land from before you, and destroy all their carved images, and destroy all their molded images, and destroy all their high places.

—NUMBERS 33:52

But if you do not drive out the inhabitants of the land from before you, then those whom you let remain will be like thorns in your eyes and thorns in your sides. They will show hostility to you in the land in which you live.

—NUMBERS 33:55

Among the cities which you will give to the Levites there will be six cities of refuge, which you will appoint for the manslayer, that he may flee there, and to them you will add forty-two cities.

—NUMBERS 35:6

Then you shall designate cities as your cities of refuge, so that a manslayer who unintentionally kills a person may flee there.

—Numbers 35:11

The cities will be for you a refuge from the avenger, so that the manslayer does not die until he stands trial before the assembly.

—Numbers 35:12

The cities which you designate shall be your six cities of refuge.

—Numbers 35:13

You will give three cities across the Jordan, and three cities you will give in the land of Canaan, which will be cities of refuge.

—Numbers 35:14

For the children of Israel, and for the stranger, and for the foreign sojourner among them will be six cities. These will be for a refuge. Everyone that unintentionally kills any person may flee there.

—Numbers 35:15

And the assembly will deliver the manslayer out of the hand of the avenger of blood, and the assembly will restore him to the city of his refuge where he fled, and he will dwell in it until the death of the high priest, who was anointed with the holy oil.

—Numbers 35:25

Deuteronomy

The Lord your God who goes before you, He shall fight for you, just as all that He did for you in Egypt before your eyes.

—Deuteronomy 1:30

Do not fear them, for the Lord your God, He shall fight for you.

—Deuteronomy 3:22

...to drive out nations from before you greater and mightier than you are, to bring you in, to give you their land for an inheritance, as it is today.

—Deuteronomy 4:38

I am the Lord, your God, who brought you out of the land of Egypt, from the house of bondage.

—Deuteronomy 5:6

...to drive out all your enemies before you, just as the Lord has spoken.

—Deuteronomy 6:19

When the Lord your God brings you into the land which you are entering to possess and has driven out many nations before you, the Hittites and the Girgashites and the Amorites and the Canaanites and the Perizzites and the Hivites and the Jebusites, seven nations greater and mightier than you...

—Deuteronomy 7:1

But the Lord your God will deliver them to you and will throw them into a great confusion until they are destroyed.

—Deuteronomy 7:23

He will deliver their kings into your hand so that you may erase their names from under heaven. No man will be able to stand before you until you have destroyed them.

—Deuteronomy 7:24

Do not say in your heart, after the Lord your God has driven them out before you, "On account of my righteousness the Lord has brought me in to possess this land," but it is because of the wickedness of these nations the Lord is driving them out before you.

—Deuteronomy 9:4

At the end of every seven years you shall grant a relinquishing of debts. This is the manner of the relinquishing: Every creditor that has loaned anything to his neighbor shall relinquish it. He shall not exact it of his neighbor, or of his brother, because it is called the Lord's relinquishment.

—Deuteronomy 15:1–2

If your brother, a Hebrew man, or a Hebrew woman, is sold to you and serves you six years, then in the seventh year you must let him go free from you. When you send him out free from you, you must not let him go away empty-handed. You shall supply him liberally out of your flock, out of your floor, and out of your winepress. From that with which the LORD your God has blessed you, you shall give to him.

—DEUTERONOMY 15:12–14

There must not be found among you anyone who makes his son or his daughter pass through the fire, or who uses divination, or uses witchcraft, or an interpreter of omens, or a sorcerer.

—DEUTERONOMY 18:10

For the LORD your God is He that goes with you, to fight for you against your enemies, to save you.

—DEUTERONOMY 20:4

For these nations, which you shall possess, listened to soothsayers and to diviners, but as for you, the LORD your God has not permitted you to do so.

—DEUTERONOMY 18:14

Then the LORD your God will overturn your captivity and have compassion on you and will return and gather you from all the nations, where the LORD your God has scattered you.

—DEUTERONOMY 30:3

They sacrificed to demons, not to God, to gods whom they knew not, to new gods that recently came along, whom your fathers did not fear.

—DEUTERONOMY 32:17

How should one chase a thousand, and two put ten thousand to flight, unless their Rock had sold them, and the LORD had given them up?

—DEUTERONOMY 32:30

Joshua

They said to Joshua, "The LORD has surely given the whole land into our hands! Indeed, all the inhabitants of the land melt in terror before us."

—JOSHUA 2:24

On the day the LORD gave over the Amorites to the children of Israel, Joshua spoke to the LORD and said in full view of Israel: "Sun, stand still over Gibeon; and moon, in the Valley of Aijalon." So the sun stood still, and the moon stood in place until the people brought vengeance on their enemies. Is this not written in the book of Jashar? The sun stood still in the middle of the sky and did not set for about a full day.

—JOSHUA 10:12–13

As for you, do not stop pursuing your enemies, but attack them from behind. Do not let them go back to their cities, for the LORD your God has given them into your hand.

—JOSHUA 10:19

When they brought out those five kings to Joshua, he called out to all the men of Israel and the army commanders, "Come here and place your feet on the necks of these kings." So they came near and placed their feet on their necks.

—Joshua 10:24

So Joshua attacked the whole land: the hill country, the Negev, the lowlands, the mountain slopes, and all their kings. No survivor was left. He destroyed all who breathed, as the Lord God of Israel had commanded.

—Joshua 10:40

Joshua captured all these kings and their land in one campaign because the Lord God of Israel waged war for Israel.

—Joshua 10:42

Joshua captured all these kings and their towns. He struck with the edge of the sword, destroying them, as Moses the servant of the Lord had commanded.

—Joshua 11:12

Joshua engaged all those kings in battle for a long time.

—Joshua 11:18

At that time Joshua came and wiped out the Anakites from the hill country: from Hebron, from Debir, from Anab, from all the hill country of Judah, and from all the hill country of Israel. Joshua utterly destroyed them and their cities.

—Joshua 11:21

And in Bashan all the kingdom of Og, one of the last remnant of the giants, who reigned in

Ashtaroth and Edrei. Moses struck them down and took their lands.

—JOSHUA 13:12

So now, give me this hill country that the LORD spoke about on that day. That day you heard that the Anakites live there in large, fortified cities. Perhaps the LORD will be with me, and I will drive them out, as the LORD said.

—JOSHUA 14:12

Caleb drove out from there three Anakites: Sheshai, Ahiman, and Talmai, descendants of Anak.

—JOSHUA 15:14

The LORD gave them rest all around, according to all that He swore to their fathers. Not a man among their enemies stood before them, and the LORD delivered all their enemies into their hands.

—JOSHUA 21:44

One man from among you can make a thousand flee, for it is the LORD your God who wages war for you, as He told you.

—JOSHUA 23:10

I sent Moses and Aaron, I struck Egypt down with all I did in their midst, and afterward I brought you out. I brought your fathers out of Egypt, then you came to the sea. The Egyptians pursued your fathers with chariots and horsemen to the Red Sea. Your fathers cried out to the LORD, and He placed darkness between you and the Egyptians. He made the sea come upon them and cover them. Your own eyes saw what I did to Egypt, and you lived in the wilderness a long time.

—JOSHUA 24:5–7

Judges

The LORD said, "Judah shall go up. Indeed, I have given the land into their hands."

—JUDGES 1:2

Then Judah went up, and the LORD gave the Canaanites and Perizzites into their hands. They struck down ten thousand men in Bezek.

—JUDGES 1:4

Then the LORD raised up judges who delivered them from the hand of those who plundered them.

—JUDGES 2:16

When the LORD raised up judges for them, the LORD was with the judge and delivered them from the hand of their enemies all the days of the judge; for their groaning before their oppressors and tormentors grieved the LORD.

—JUDGES 2:18

The Spirit of the LORD came on him, and he judged Israel. He went out to battle, and the LORD gave Cushan-Rishathaim, king of Mesopotamia, into his hands, so that Othniel overpowered Cushan-Rishathaim.

—JUDGES 3:10

Then the children of Israel cried out to the LORD, and the LORD raised up a deliverer—Ehud son of

Gera the Benjamite, a left-handed man. The children of Israel sent a tribute payment by him to King Eglon of Moab.

—Judges 3:15

After Ehud was Shamgar son of Anath. He struck down six hundred Philistine men with an ox goad. He also saved Israel.

—Judges 3:31

Then Deborah said to Barak, "Get up, for this is the day that the Lord has given Sisera into your hands. Has not the Lord gone out before you?" So Barak went down from Mount Tabor with ten thousand men behind him.

—Judges 4:14

The Lord said to Gideon, "With three hundred men who lapped to drink, I will save you and give the Midianites into your hands. All the rest of the people should go home."

—Judges 7:7

So Jephthah crossed over to the Ammonites to wage war against them, and the Lord gave them into his hands.

—Judges 11:32

1 Samuel

For rebellion is as the sin of witchcraft, and stubbornness is as iniquity and idolatry. Because you have rejected the word of the Lord, He has also rejected you from being king.

—1 Samuel 15:23

Then David said to the Philistine, "You come to me with a sword, a spear, and a shield, but I come to you in the name of the LORD of Hosts, the God of the armies of Israel, whom you have reviled. This day will the LORD deliver you into my hand. And I will strike you down and cut off your head. Then I will give the corpses of the Philistine camp this day to the birds of the air and to the beasts of the earth so that all the earth may know that there is a God in Israel. And then all this assembly will know that it is not by sword and spear that the LORD saves. For the battle belongs to the LORD, and He will give you into our hands."

When the Philistine arose and came near to meet David, David hurried and ran toward the battle line to meet the Philistine. David put his hand in his bag and took from there a stone. And he slung it and struck the Philistine in his forehead. Therefore the stone sunk into his forehead and he fell upon his face to the ground.

So David prevailed over the Philistine with a sling and with a stone. And he struck down the Philistine and slew him, but there was no sword in the hand of David. Therefore David ran and stood over the Philistine. Then he took his sword and drew it from out of its sheath, and he finished him off and he cut off his head with it.

When the Philistines saw their champion was dead, they fled.

—1 SAMUEL 17:45–51

David inquired at the LORD, saying, "Should I pursue after this raiding party? Will I overtake them?" And He answered him, "Pursue them, for you will surely overtake them and will surely recover all."

—1 Samuel 30:8

2 Samuel

Now afterwards there was again a battle with the Philistines at Gob. Then Sibbekai the Hushathite struck down Saph, who was among the descendants of the giant.

—2 Samuel 21:18

Once again, there was a battle with the Philistines at Gob. On this occasion, Elhanan the son of Jaare-Oregim the Bethlehemite struck down Goliath the Gittite, whose spear shaft was like a weaver's beam. Once again, there was war at Gath. There was a man of stature who had six fingers on each hand and six toes on each foot, twenty-four in number. Now he also was born to the giant. When he taunted Israel, Jonathan the son of Shimeah, the brother of David, struck him down. Now these four were born to the giant in Gath, and they fell by the hand of David and by the hand of his servants.

—2 Samuel 21:19–22

He said: The LORD is my rock and my fortress and my deliverer.

—2 Samuel 22:2

He rescued me from my strong enemy, from those who hate me; for they were stronger than I.

—2 SAMUEL 22:18

He brought me to the open expanse; He rescued me, for He delighted in me.

—2 SAMUEL 22:20

Who brought me out from my enemies. You exalted me above those who rose up against me; You delivered me from violent ones.

—2 SAMUEL 22:49

1 Kings

There were also male cult prostitutes in the land, and they did according to all the abominations of the nations that the LORD cast out before the children of Israel.

—1 KINGS 14:24

He performed the most abominable act in following idols like the Amorites, whom the LORD cast out before the children of Israel.

—1 KINGS 21:26

2 Kings

When Joram saw Jehu he said, "Is it peace, Jehu?" And he said, "What peace, so long as the harlotries of your mother Jezebel and her sorceries are so many?"

—2 KINGS 9:22

1 Chronicles

And they went up to Baal Perazim, and David struck them down there. Then David said, "God broke through my enemies by my hand as the breaking through of waters." Therefore they named that place Baal Perazim.

—1 Chronicles 14:11

2 Chronicles

And he set for himself priests for the high places and for the goat and calf idols that he made.

—2 Chronicles 11:15

He even made his sons pass through the fire in the Valley of Ben Hinnom; and he had conjurers, and practitioners of divination and sorcery, and necromancers, and mediums. So he did a great amount of evil in the eyes of the Lord, so that God was provoked.

—2 Chronicles 33:6

Esther

For if you remain silent at this time, protection and deliverance for the Jews will be ordained from some other place, but you and your father's house shall be destroyed. And who knows if you may have attained royal position for such a time as this?

—Esther 4:14

Job

I broke the jaws of the wicked and plucked the victim from his teeth.

—Job 29:17

And the Lord restored the fortunes of Job when he prayed for his friends, and also the Lord gave Job twice as much as he had before.

—Job 42:10

Psalms

Arise, O Lord; save me, O my God! For You have struck all my enemies on the cheek; You have broken the teeth of the wicked.

—Psalm 3:7

Declare them guilty, O God; may they fall by their own counsels; cast them out in the multitude of their transgressions, for they have rebelled against You.

—Psalm 5:10

Return, O Lord, rescue my soul. Save me for the sake of Your lovingkindness.

—Psalm 6:4

O Lord my God, in You I put my trust; save me from all those who persecute me, and deliver me.

—Psalm 7:1

Lest they tear my soul like a lion, rending it in pieces, while there is none to deliver.

—Psalm 7:2

The Lord also will be a refuge for the oppressed, a refuge in times of trouble.

—Psalm 9:9

Oh, that the salvation of Israel would come from Zion! When the Lord turns back the captivity of His people, Jacob will rejoice, and Israel will be glad.

—Psalm 14:7

Arise, O Lord! Confront him, cast him down! Deliver my soul from the wicked by Your sword.

—Psalm 17:13

The Lord is my pillar, and my fortress, and my deliverer; my God, my rock, in whom I take refuge; my shield, and the horn of my salvation, my high tower.

—Psalm 18:2

I will call on the Lord, who is worthy to be praised, and I will be saved from my enemies.

—Psalm 18:3

He sent from above, He took me; He drew me out of many waters.

—Psalm 18:16

He delivered me from my strong enemy, and from those who hated me, for they were too strong for me.

—Psalm 18:17

He also brought me forth into a large place; He delivered me because He delighted in me.

—Psalm 18:19

For You will save the afflicted people, but will bring down prideful eyes.

—Psalm 18:27

He trains my hands for war, so that my arms bend a bow of bronze.

—Psalm 18:34

You gave me the necks of my enemies, and I destroyed those who hate me.

—Psalm 18:40

Then I beat them small as the dust before the wind; I cast them out as the dirt in the streets.

—Psalm 18:42

He gives great deliverance to His king, and shows lovingkindness to His anointed, to David and to his descendants for evermore.

—Psalm 18:50

Rescue my soul from the sword, my only life from the power of the dog.

—Psalm 22:20

Save me from the lion's mouth, and from the horns of the wild ox, answer me!

—Psalm 22:21

For He has not despised nor abhorred the affliction of the afflicted; nor has He hid His face from him; but when he cried to Him, He heard.

—Psalm 22:24

He restores my soul; He leads me in paths of righteousness for His name's sake.

—Psalm 23:3

O my God, I trust in You; may I not be ashamed; may my enemies not triumph over me.

—Psalm 25:2

Watch over my life, and deliver me! Let me not suffer shame, for I seek refuge in You.

—Psalm 25:20

The Lord is my light and my salvation; whom will I fear? The Lord is the strength of my life; of whom will I be afraid?

—Psalm 27:1

When the wicked came against me to eat my flesh my enemies and my foes—they stumbled and fell.

—Psalm 27:2

In You, O Lord, do I seek refuge; may I never be ashamed; deliver me in Your righteousness.

—Psalm 31:1

Incline Your ear to me; deliver me speedily; be my strong rock, a strong fortress to save me.

—Psalm 31:2

My times are in Your hand; deliver me from the hand of my enemies and my pursuers.

—Psalm 31:15

You are my hiding place; You will preserve me from trouble; You will surround me with shouts of deliverance. Selah.

—Psalm 32:7

To deliver their soul from death, and to keep them alive in famine.

—Psalm 33:19

I sought the Lord, and he heard me, and delivered me from all my fears.

—Psalm 34:4

I sought the Lord, and He answered me, and delivered me from all my fears.

—Psalm 34:7

The righteous cry out, and the Lord hears, and delivers them out of all their troubles.

—Psalm 34:17

The Lord is near to the broken-hearted, and saves the contrite of spirit.

—Psalm 34:18

Many are the afflictions of the righteous, but the Lord delivers him out of them all.

—Psalm 34:19

Plead my cause, O Lord, with my adversaries; fight those who fight me.

—Psalm 35:1

All my bones will say, "Lord, who is like You, who delivers the poor from a stronger one, the poor and the needy from the one who robs them?"

—Psalm 35:10

But the wicked will perish, and the enemies of the Lord will be like the glory of pastures; they will waste away, in smoke they will waste away.

—Psalm 37:20

The Lord will help them and deliver them; He will deliver them from the wicked, and save them, because they take refuge in Him.

—Psalm 37:40

Make haste to help me, O Lord, my salvation.

—Psalm 38:22

He also brought me up out of a horrible pit, out of the miry clay, and set my feet on a rock, and established my steps.

—Psalm 40:2

Be pleased, O Lord, to deliver me; O Lord, make haste to help me.

—Psalm 40:13

But I am poor and needy; yet the Lord thinks about me. You are my help and my deliverer; do not delay, O my God.

—Psalm 40:17

Blessed are those who consider the poor; the Lord will deliver them in the day of trouble.

—Psalm 41:1

The LORD will preserve them and keep them alive, and they will be blessed on the earth, and You will not deliver them to the will of their enemies.

—PSALM 41:2

You are my King, O God; command deliverances for Jacob.

—PSALM 44:4

Through You we will push down our opponents; through Your name we will trample those who rise up against us.

—PSALM 44:5

But You have saved us from our opponents, and have put to shame those who hate us.

—PSALM 44:7

And call on Me in the day of trouble; I will deliver you, and you will glorify Me.

—PSALM 50:15

Now consider this, you who forget God, lest I tear you in pieces, and there be none to deliver.

—PSALM 50:22

Restore to me the joy of Your salvation, and uphold me with Your willing spirit.

—PSALM 51:12

The sacrifices of God are a broken spirit; a broken and a contrite heart, O God, You will not despise.

—PSALM 51:17

Break their teeth in their mouth, O God; break out the great teeth of the young lions, O Lord.

—Psalm 58:6

Say to God, "How awesome are Your works! Through the greatness of Your power Your enemies cringe before You."

—Psalm 66:3

Let God arise, let His enemies be scattered; let those who hate Him flee before Him.

—Psalm 68:1

God sets the deserted in families; He brings out prisoners into prosperity, but the rebellious dwell in a dry land.

—Psalm 68:6

Save me, O God! For the waters have come up to my throat.

—Psalm 69:1

Deliver me out of the mire that I may not sink; may I be delivered from those who hate me, and out of the watery depths.

—Psalm 69:14

May the stream not overflow me; neither may the deep swallow me up, nor the pit close its mouth on me.

—Psalm 69:15

Draw near to my soul, and redeem it; deliver me because of my enemies.

—Psalm 69:18

For the LORD hears the poor, and does not despise His prisoners.

—PSALM 69:33

Make haste, O God, to deliver me! Make haste to help me, O LORD.

—PSALM 70:1

But I am poor and needy; make haste to me, O God! You are my help and my deliverer; O LORD, do not delay!

—PSALM 70:5

Deliver me in Your righteousness and help me escape; incline Your ear to me and save me.

—PSALM 71:2

Deliver me, O my God, out of the hand of the wicked, out of the hand of the unjust and cruel man.

—PSALM 71:4

O God, do not be far from me; O my God, act quickly to help me.

—PSALM 71:12

May those who dwell in the wilderness bow before him, and his enemies lick the dust.

—PSALM 72:9

Indeed, may he deliver the needy when he cries; the poor also, and him who has no helper.

—PSALM 72:12

For God is my King of old, working salvation in the midst of the earth.

—PSALM 74:12

You divided the sea by Your strength; You broke the heads of the dragons on the waters.

—PSALM 74:13

Let the groans of the prisoners come before You; according to the greatness of Your power preserve those who are appointed to die.

—PSALM 79:11

You called in trouble, and I delivered you; I answered you in the secret place of thunder; I tested you at the waters of Meribah. Selah.

—PSALM 81:7

Grant escape to the abused and the destitute, pluck them out of the hand of the false.

—PSALM 82:4

LORD, You have been favorable to Your land; You have brought back the captivity of Jacob.

—PSALM 85:1

For great is Your mercy toward me, and You have delivered my soul from the depths of Sheol.

—PSALM 86:13

Show me a sign of Your favor, that those who hate me may see it and be ashamed because You, LORD, have helped and comforted me.

—PSALM 86:17

You crushed Rahab like a corpse; You scattered Your enemies with Your strong arm.

—PSALM 89:10

I will beat down his foes before him and strike down those who hate him.

—PSALM 89:23

Surely He shall deliver you from the snare of the hunter and from the deadly pestilence.

—PSALM 91:3

You shall tread upon the lion and adder; the young lion and the serpent you shall trample underfoot.

—PSALM 91:13

Because he has set his love upon Me, therefore I will deliver him; I will set him on high, because he has known My name.

—PSALM 91:14

He shall call upon Me, and I will answer him; I will be with him in trouble, and I will deliver him and honor him.

—PSALM 91:15

A fire goes before Him and burns up His enemies all around.

—PSALM 97:3

You who love the LORD, hate evil! He preserves the lives of His devoted ones; He delivers them from the hand of the wicked.

—PSALM 97:10

For He has looked down from the height of His sanctuary; from heaven the LORD looked down on the earth, to hear the groaning of the prisoners and to set free those who are appointed to death.

—Psalm 102:19–20

The king sent and released him; the ruler of the people let him go free.

—Psalm 105:20

He rebuked the Red Sea, and it was dried up, so He led them through the depths as through the wilderness.

—Psalm 106:9

He saved them from the hand of him who hated them and redeemed them from the hand of the enemy.

—Psalm 106:10

The waters covered their enemies; there was not one of them left.

—Psalm 106:11

Yes, they sacrificed their sons and their daughters to demons.

—Psalm 106:37

Then they cried unto the Lord in their trouble, and He delivered them out of their distresses.

—Psalm 107:6

For He satisfies the longing soul and fills the hungry soul with goodness. Some sit in darkness and in the shadow of death, being prisoners in affliction and irons, because they rebelled against the words of God and rejected the counsel of the Most High.

—Psalm 107:9–11

Some were fools because of their transgressions, and because of their iniquities they are afflicted.

—Psalm 107:17

He sent His word and healed them and delivered them from their destruction.

—Psalm 107:20

That Your beloved ones may be delivered, provide salvation with Your right hand and answer me.

—Psalm 108:6

Help me, O Lord my God! Save me according to Your mercy.

—Psalm 109:26

The Lord shall send your mighty scepter out of Zion; rule in the midst of your enemies.

—Psalm 110:2

Then called I upon the name of the Lord: "O Lord, I plead with You, deliver my soul."

—Psalm 116:4

For You have delivered my soul from death, my eyes from tears, and my feet from falling.

—Psalm 116:8

O Lord, I am Your servant; I am Your servant, the son of Your female servant; You have loosed my bonds.

—Psalm 116:16

The Lord is on my side to help me; I shall look in triumph upon those who hate me.

—Psalm 118:7

I shall not die, but I shall live and declare the works of the Lord.

—Psalm 118:17

Deliver me from the oppression of man, so I will keep Your precepts.

—Psalm 119:134

Consider my affliction, and deliver me, for I do not forget Your law.

—Psalm 119:153

Plead my cause, and defend me; revive me according to Your word.

—Psalm 119:154

Let my supplication come before You; deliver me according to Your word.

—Psalm 119:170

Deliver my soul, O Lord, from lying lips and from a deceitful tongue.

—Psalm 120:2

Blessed be the Lord, who has not given us for a prey to their teeth.

—Psalm 124:6

We have escaped as a bird out of the snare of the hunters; the snare is broken, and we have escaped.

—Psalm 124:7

When the Lord restored the captives of Zion, we were like those who dream.

—Psalm 126:1

Restore our captives, O Lord, as the streams in the Negev.

—Psalm 126:4

Let all those be shamed and turned back who hate Zion.

—Psalm 129:5

...to Him who divided the Red Sea into two, for His mercy endures forever; and made Israel to pass through the midst of it, for His mercy endures forever; but overthrew Pharaoh and his host in the Red Sea, for His mercy endures forever.

—Psalm 136:13–15

Though I walk in the midst of trouble, You will preserve me; You stretch forth Your hand against the wrath of my enemies, and Your right hand saves me.

—Psalm 138:7

Deliver me, O Lord, from evil men; protect me from violent men.

—Psalm 140:1

Attend to my cry, for I am brought very low; deliver me from my persecutors, for they are stronger than me.

—Psalm 142:6

Bring my soul out of prison, that I may praise Your name; the righteous shall surround me, for You shall deal bountifully with me.

—Psalm 142:7

Respond to me quickly, O Lord, my spirit fails; do not hide Your face from me, lest I be like those who go down into the pit.

—Psalm 143:7

In Your mercy cut off my enemies, and destroy all them who afflict my soul, for I am Your servant.

—Psalm 143:12

Deliver me, O Lord, from my enemies; I flee unto You for my protection.

—Psalm 143:9

Blessed be the Lord my strength, who prepares my hands for war, and my fingers to fight.

—Psalm 144:1

…my goodness, and my fortress; my high tower, and my deliverer, my shield, and in whom I trust; who subdues nations under me.

—Psalm 144:2

Send Your hand from above; rescue me, and deliver me out of the great waters, from the hand of foreigners.

—PSALM 144:7

It is He who gives victory to kings, who delivers David His servant from the cruel sword.

—PSALM 144:10

Rescue me and deliver me from the hand of foreigners, whose mouths speak lies and whose right hand is a right hand of falsehood.

—PSALM 144:11

...who executes justice for the oppressed, who gives food to the hungry. The LORD releases the prisoners.

—PSALM 146:7

...to bind their kings with chains, and their nobles with shackles of iron.

—PSALM 149:8

Proverbs

...to deliver you from the way of the evil man, from the man who speaks perverse things...

—PROVERBS 2:12

...to deliver you from the immoral woman, even from the seductress who flatters with her words...

—PROVERBS 2:16

The spirit of a man will sustain his infirmity, but a wounded spirit who can bear?

—PROVERBS 18:14

As the bird by flitting, as the swallow by flying, so the curse without cause will not alight.

—Proverbs 26:2

Ecclesiastes

He who digs a pit will fall into it, and whoever breaks through a wall will be bitten by a serpent.

—Ecclesiastes 10:8

Isaiah

There shall be a tabernacle for a shadow in the daytime from the heat, and for a place of refuge, and for a shelter from storm and from rain.

—Isaiah 4:6

In that day his burden shall be taken away from off your shoulder, and his yoke from off your neck; and the yoke shall be destroyed because of the anointing oil.

—Isaiah 10:27

For You have been a defense to the poor, a defense to the needy in his distress, a refuge from the storm, a shadow from the heat; for the breath of the ruthless ones is as a storm against the wall.

—Isaiah 25:4

In that day the Lord with His fierce and great and strong sword shall punish Leviathan the fleeing serpent, even Leviathan the twisted serpent; and He shall slay the dragon that is in the sea.

—Isaiah 27:1

Your covenant with death shall be annulled, and your agreement with hell shall not stand; when the overflowing scourge passes through, then you shall be trodden down by it.

—Isaiah 28:18

...to open the blind eyes, to bring out the prisoners from the prison, and those who sit in darkness out of the prison house.

—Isaiah 42:7

The Lord shall go forth like a mighty man; He shall stir up zeal like a man of war. He shall cry out, yes, raise a war cry; He shall prevail against His enemies.

—Isaiah 42:13

But this is a people robbed and despoiled; they are all snared in holes, and they are hidden in prison houses; they are for a prey, and no one delivers, for a spoil, and no one says, "Restore them."

—Isaiah 42:22

...who frustrates the omens of the boasters and makes fools out of diviners, who turns wise men backward and makes their knowledge foolish...

—Isaiah 44:25

I have raised him up in righteousness, and I will direct all his ways; he shall build My city, and he shall let My captives go, neither for price nor reward, says the Lord of Hosts.

—Isaiah 45:13

And even to your old age I am He, and even to your graying years I will carry you; I have done it, and I will bear you; even I will carry, and will deliver you.

—Isaiah 46:4

Go forth from Babylon! Flee from the Chaldeans! With a voice of singing declare, proclaim this, utter it even to the ends of the earth; say, "The Lord has redeemed His servant Jacob."

—Isaiah 48:20

…saying to the prisoners, "Go forth," to those who are in darkness, "Show yourselves." They shall feed along the paths, and their pastures shall be in all desolate heights.

—Isaiah 49:9

Sing, O heavens! And be joyful, O earth! And break forth into singing, O mountains! For the Lord has comforted His people and will have mercy on His afflicted.

—Isaiah 49:13

For thus says the Lord: Even the captives of the mighty shall be taken away, and the prey of the tyrant shall be delivered; for I will contend with him who contends with you, and I will save your sons.

—Isaiah 49:25

Awake, awake, put on strength, O arm of the Lord. Awake as in the ancient days, in the generations of old. Was it not You who cut Rahab to pieces and wounded the dragon?

—Isaiah 51:9

Shake yourself from the dust; arise, O captive Jerusalem. Loose yourself from the bonds of your neck, O captive daughter of Zion.

—ISAIAH 52:2

But he was wounded for our transgressions, he was bruised for our iniquities; the chastisement of our peace was upon him, and by his stripes we are healed.

—ISAIAH 53:5

O afflicted one, tossed with tempest and not comforted, I will lay your stones with fair colors and lay your foundations with sapphires.

—ISAIAH 54:11

For thus says the High and Lofty One who inhabits eternity, whose name is Holy: I dwell in the high and holy place and also with him who is of a contrite and humble spirit, to revive the spirit of the humble, and to revive the heart of the contrite ones.

—ISAIAH 57:15

Is not this the fast that I have chosen: to loose the bonds of wickedness, to undo the heavy burdens, and to let the oppressed go free, and break every yoke?

—ISAIAH 58:6

So shall they fear the name of the LORD from the west and His glory from the rising of the sun; when the enemy shall come in like a flood, the Spirit of the LORD shall lift up a standard against him.

—ISAIAH 59:19

The Spirit of the Lord GOD is upon me because the LORD has anointed me to preach good news to the poor; He has sent me to heal the broken-hearted, to proclaim liberty to the captives, and the opening of the prison to those who are bound.

—ISAIAH 61:1

In all their affliction He was afflicted, and the angel of His presence saved them; in His love and in His mercy He redeemed them; and He lifted them and carried them all the days of old.

—ISAIAH 63:9

For My hand made all those things, thus all those things have come to be, says the LORD. But to this man I will look, even to him who is poor and of a contrite spirit, and trembles at My word.

—ISAIAH 66:2

Jeremiah

They have healed also the brokenness of the daughter of My people superficially, saying, "Peace, peace," when there is no peace.

—JEREMIAH 6:14

For they have healed the brokenness of the daughter of My people superficially, saying, "Peace, peace," when there is no peace.

—JEREMIAH 8:11

For thus says the LORD: When seventy years have been completed for Babylon, I will visit you and perform My good word toward you, in causing you to return to this place.

—JEREMIAH 29:10

…that every man should let his male slave and every man his female slave, being a Hebrew man or a Hebrew woman, go free so that no one should keep them, a Jew his brother, in bondage.

—JEREMIAH 34:9

He says: You are My battle-ax and weapon of war: for with you I will break in pieces the nations, and with you I will destroy kingdoms.

—JEREMIAH 51:20

Daniel

If it be so, our God whom we serve is able to deliver us from the burning fiery furnace, and He will deliver us out of your hand, O king.

—DANIEL 3:17

Then Nebuchadnezzar came near to the mouth of the burning fiery furnace, and spoke, and said, "Shadrach, Meshach, and Abednego, you servants of the Most High God, come out and come here!"

Then Shadrach, Meshach, and Abednego came out of the midst of the fire.

—Daniel 3:26

My God has sent His angel and has shut the lions' mouths so that they have not hurt me, because innocence was found in me before Him; and also before you, O king, I have done no harm.

—Daniel 6:22

Then he said to me, "Do not be afraid, Daniel. For from the first day that you set your heart to understand this and to humble yourself before your God, your words were heard, and I have come because of your words. But the prince of the kingdom of Persia withstood me for twenty-one days. So Michael, one of the chief princes, came to help me, for I had been left there with the kings of Persia."

—Daniel 10:12–13

Joel

And I will compensate you for the years the locusts have eaten—the larval locust, the hopper locust, and the fledging locust—My great army which I sent against you.

—Joel 2:25

And it will be that everyone who calls on the name of the Lord will be saved. For on Mount Zion and in Jerusalem there will be deliverance, as the

Lord has said, and among the survivors whom the Lord calls.

—Joel 2:32

Obadiah

But on Mount Zion there shall be deliverance, and it shall be holy; and the house of Jacob shall possess those who dispossessed them.

—Obadiah 1:17

Saviors shall go up to Mount Zion to rule Mount Esau, and the kingdom shall be the Lord's.

—Obadiah 1:21

Micah

Then I will cut off sorceries from your hand, and you will no longer have fortune-tellers.

—Micah 5:12

Nahum

Because of the countless harlotries of the seductive harlot, the mistress of sorceries, who sells nations through her harlotries and families through her sorceries.

—Nahum 3:4

Zechariah

And the Lord said to Satan, "The Lord rebuke you, Satan! The Lord who has chosen Jerusalem rebukes you! Is this not a burning brand taken out of the fire?"

—Zechariah 3:2

For the household Teraphim idols speak wickedness, and the diviners envision lies. They utter false dreams, and provide comfort that does not last. So the people wander about like sheep; they are afflicted because there is no shepherd.

—Zechariah 10:2

My anger burns against the shepherds, and I will visit judgment on the male goats. For the Lord of Hosts will visit His flock, the house of Judah, and will make them like His majestic horse in battle.

—Zechariah 10:3

Malachi

But for you who fear My name, the sun of righteousness will rise with healing in its wings. You will go out and grow up like calves from the stall.

—Malachi 4:2

6

DELIVERANCE IN THE
NEW TESTAMENT

THE DELIVERER HAS come to the earth. Through the New Testament we see God's deliverance come to man not only physically—winning physical battles over physical enemies—but now we also see His deliverance in the spiritual realm. From the Son of God Himself we learn how to gain victory, once and for all, over the enemy of our souls. Jesus shows us the spiritual weapons that are at our disposal. He shows us that He has the keys of the kingdom, which represent authority, and we learn that He has given those keys to us. Through Christ not only do we have physical victory, but we also have victory over all the works of the enemy—and nothing shall by any means hurt us.

In this half of the Bible, Christ also introduces us to the third member of the Godhead, the Comforter, the Holy Spirit, who will teach us all the ways of the abundant life and how to walk in the peace, joy, and righteousness of the kingdom of God. We are invited to be filled with the Spirit of God, that not only will we be saved, healed, and delivered ourselves, but also we will have power to expand God's kingdom of peace by reconciling others to Him.

Through the Holy Spirit we have access to an unlimited measure of supernatural grace and wisdom and spiritual resources that allow us to truly live as the priests, as saints, in the kingdom of God. The devil has no power over the saints of God. This is the age we live in, an age when Christ has come, has died, is risen, and is now at the right hand of the Father.

Matthew

His fame went throughout all Syria. And they brought to Him all sick people who were taken with various diseases and tormented with pain, those who were possessed with demons, those who had seizures, and those who had paralysis, and He healed them.

—Matthew 4:24

And lead us not into temptation, but deliver us from evil. For Yours is the kingdom and the power and the glory forever. Amen.

—Matthew 6:13

You hypocrite! First take the plank out of your own eye, and then you will see clearly to take the speck out of your brother's eye.

—Matthew 7:5

Not everyone who says to Me, "Lord, Lord," shall enter the kingdom of heaven, but he who does the will of My Father who is in heaven. Many will say to Me on that day, "Lord, Lord, have we not prophesied in Your name, cast out demons in Your name, and done many wonderful works in Your name?" But then I will declare to them, "I never knew you. Depart from Me, you who practice evil."

—MATTHEW 7:21–23

When the evening came, they brought to Him many who were possessed with demons. And He cast out the spirits with His word, and healed all who were sick.

—MATTHEW 8:16

When He came to the other side into the country of the Gergesenes, there met Him two men possessed with demons, coming out of the tombs, extremely fierce, so that no one might pass by that way.

—MATTHEW 8:28

Those who kept them fled, and went their ways into the city, and told everything, including what had happened to those possessed by the demons.

—MATTHEW 8:33

As they went out, they brought to Him a mute man possessed with a demon.

—MATTHEW 9:32

And when the demon was cast out, the mute man spoke, and the crowds were amazed, saying, "This has never been seen in Israel."

—Matthew 9:33

He called His twelve disciples to Him and gave them authority over unclean spirits, to cast them out, and to heal all kinds of sickness and all kinds of disease.

—Matthew 10:1

Heal the sick, cleanse the lepers, raise the dead, cast out devils: freely ye have received, freely give.

—Matthew 10:8, kjv

Then one possessed with a demon was brought to Him, blind and mute, and He healed him, so that the blind and mute man both spoke and saw.

—Matthew 12:22

All the people were amazed and said, "Is He not the Son of David?" But when the Pharisees heard it, they said, "This Man does not cast out demons, except by Beelzebub the ruler of the demons." Jesus knew their thoughts and said to them, "Every kingdom divided against itself is brought to desolation. And every city or house divided against itself will not stand. If Satan casts out Satan, he is divided against himself. Then how will his kingdom stand?"

—Matthew 12:23–26

But if I cast out demons by the Spirit of God, then the kingdom of God has come upon you.

—Matthew 12:28

When an unclean spirit goes out of a man, it passes through dry places seeking rest, but finds none.

—Matthew 12:43

There, a woman of Canaan came out of the same regions and cried out to Him, saying, "Have mercy on me, O Lord, Son of David. My daughter is severely possessed by a demon."

—Matthew 15:22

But He answered, "It is not fair to take the children's bread and to throw it to dogs." She said, "Yes, Lord, yet even dogs eat the crumbs that fall from their masters' table." Then Jesus answered her, "O woman, great is your faith. Let it be done for you as you desire." And her daughter was healed instantly.

—Matthew 15:26–28

Lord, have mercy on my son, for he is an epileptic and suffers terribly. He often falls into the fire and often into the water.

—Matthew 17:15

Jesus rebuked the demon, and he came out of him. And the child was healed instantly.

—Matthew 17:18

Mark

In their synagogue there was a man with an unclean spirit.

—MARK 1:23

When the unclean spirit had convulsed him and cried out with a loud voice, it came out of him.

—MARK 1:26

They were all amazed, so that they questioned among themselves, "What is this? What new teaching is this? With authority He commands even the unclean spirits, and they obey Him."

—MARK 1:27

In the evening, when the sun had set, they brought to Him all who were sick and those who were possessed with demons.

—MARK 1:32

And He healed many who were sick with various diseases and cast out many demons. And He did not let the demons speak, because they knew Him.

—MARK 1:34

So He preached in their synagogues throughout Galilee and cast out demons.

—MARK 1:39

When unclean spirits saw Him, they fell down before Him, crying out, "You are the Son of God."

—MARK 3:11

He ordained twelve to be with Him, and to be sent out to preach, and to have authority to heal sicknesses and to cast out demons.

—MARK 3:14–15

When He had come out of the boat, immediately a man with an unclean spirit came out of the tombs and met Him.

—MARK 5:2

Then He asked him, "What is your name?" He answered, "My name is Legion. For we are many."

—MARK 5:9

At once, Jesus gave them leave. Then the unclean spirits came out and entered the swine. And the herd, numbering about two thousand, ran wildly down a steep hill into the sea and were drowned in the sea.

—MARK 5:13

They came to Jesus and saw him who had been possessed with the legion of demons sitting and clothed and in his right mind. And they were afraid.

—MARK 5:15

When He entered the boat, he who had been possessed with the demons prayed Him that he might be with Him. Jesus did not let him, but said to him, "Go home to your friends and tell them what great things the Lord has done for you and how He has had compassion on you."

—MARK 5:18–19

And they cast out many demons and anointed with oil many who were sick and healed them.

—Mark 6:13

The woman was a Greek, a Syrophoenician by race. And she begged Him to cast the demon out of her daughter.

—Mark 7:26

Then He said to her, "For this answer, go your way. The demon has gone out of your daughter."

—Mark 7:29

When she had come to her house, she found the demon had gone out, and her daughter lying on the bed.

—Mark 7:30

Wherever it takes hold on him, it dashes him to the ground. And he foams at the mouth and gnashes with his teeth and becomes rigid. And I told Your disciples so that they would cast it out, but they could not.

—Mark 9:18

When Jesus saw that the people came running together, He rebuked the foul spirit, saying to it, "You mute and deaf spirit, I command you, come out of him, and enter him no more."

—Mark 9:25

When He had entered the house, His disciples asked Him privately, "Why could we not cast it out?" He said to them, "This kind cannot come out except by prayer and fasting."

—MARK 9:28–29

John answered Him, "Teacher, we saw one who does not follow us casting out demons in Your name, and we forbade him because he was not following us." But Jesus said, "Do not forbid him, for no one who does a miracle in My name can quickly speak evil of Me."

—MARK 9:38–39

Now when Jesus rose early on the first day of the week, He appeared first to Mary Magdalene, out of whom He had cast seven demons.

—MARK 16:9

These signs will accompany those who believe: In My name they will cast out demons; they will speak with new tongues.

—MARK 16:17

Luke

As He spoke by the mouth of His holy prophets of long ago, that we should be saved from our enemies and from the hand of all who hate us, to perform the mercy promised to our fathers and to remember His holy covenant.

—LUKE 1:70–72

The Spirit of the Lord is upon Me, because He has anointed Me to preach the gospel to the poor; He has sent Me to heal the broken-hearted, to preach deliverance to the captives and recovery of sight to the blind, to set at liberty those who are oppressed.

—Luke 4:18

In the synagogue there was a man who had the spirit of an unclean demon. And he cried out with a loud voice.

—Luke 4:33

Jesus rebuked him, saying, "Be silent, and come out of him!" When the demon had thrown him down in their midst, he came out of him and did not hurt him.

—Luke 4:35

…including those who were vexed by unclean spirits. And they were healed.

—Luke 6:18

In that same hour He cured many of their infirmities and afflictions and evil spirits. And to many who were blind He gave sight.

—Luke 7:21

…and some women who had been healed of evil spirits and infirmities: Mary, called Magdalene, from whom seven demons had come out.

—Luke 8:2

He said to them, "I saw Satan as lightning fall from heaven."

—Luke 10:18

Look, I give you authority to trample on serpents and scorpions, and over all the power of the enemy. And nothing shall by any means hurt.

—Luke 10:19

But if I cast out demons with the finger of God, no doubt the kingdom of God has come upon you.

—Luke 11:20

When Jesus saw her, He called her and said to her, "Woman, you are loosed from your infirmity."

—Luke 13:12

Then should not this woman, being a daughter of Abraham whom Satan has bound these eighteen years, be loosed from this bondage on the Sabbath?

—Luke 13:16

He said to them, "Go and tell that fox, 'Look, I cast out demons. And I perform healings today and tomorrow, and on the third day I shall be perfected.'"

—Luke 13:32

John

Therefore if the Son sets you free, you shall be free indeed.

—John 8:36

You are of your father the devil, and you want to do the desires of your father. He was a murderer from the beginning, and does not stand in the truth, because there is no truth in him. When he lies, he speaks from his own nature, for he is a liar and the father of lies.

—JOHN 8:44

He who was dead came out, his hands and feet wrapped with grave clothes, and his face wrapped with a cloth. Jesus said to them, "Unbind him, and let him go."

—JOHN 11:44

Acts

Crowds also came out of the cities surrounding Jerusalem, bringing the sick and those who were afflicted by evil spirits, and they were all healed.

—ACTS 5:16

But during the night an angel of the Lord opened the prison doors and led them out.

—ACTS 5:19

He led them out after he had shown wonders and signs in the land of Egypt, and at the Red Sea, and for forty years in the wilderness.

—ACTS 7:36

For unclean spirits, crying with a loud voice, came out of many who were possessed. And many who were paralyzed or lame were healed.

—ACTS 8:7

How God anointed Jesus of Nazareth with the Holy Spirit and with power, who went about doing good and healing all who were oppressed by the devil, for God was with Him.

—Acts 10:38

You son of the devil, enemy of all righteousness, full of deceit and of all fraud, will you not cease perverting the right ways of the Lord?

—Acts 13:10

On one occasion, as we went to the place of prayer, a servant girl possessed with a spirit of divination met us, who brought her masters much profit by fortune-telling. She followed Paul and us, shouting, "These men are servants of the Most High God, who proclaim to us the way of salvation." She did this for many days. But becoming greatly troubled, Paul turned to the spirit and said, "I command you in the name of Jesus Christ to come out of her." And it came out at that moment.

—Acts 16:16–18

At midnight Paul and Silas were praying and singing hymns to God, and the prisoners were listening to them. Suddenly there was a great earthquake, so that the foundations of the prison were shaken. And immediately all the doors were opened and everyone's shackles were loosened.

—Acts 16:25–26

So handkerchiefs or aprons he had touched were brought to the sick, and the diseases left them, and the evil spirits went out of them.

—Acts 19:12

Then some of the itinerant Jewish exorcists invoked the name of the Lord Jesus over those who had evil spirits, saying, "We command you to come out in the name of Jesus whom Paul preaches." There were seven sons of a Jewish high priest named Sceva doing this. The evil spirit answered, "I know Jesus, and I know Paul, but who are you?" Then the man in whom the evil spirit was jumped on them, overpowered them, and prevailed against them, so that they fled from that house naked and wounded.

—Acts 19:13–16

Romans

For you have not received the spirit of slavery again to fear. But you have received the Spirit of adoption, by whom we cry, "Abba, Father."

—Romans 8:15

The God of peace will soon crush Satan under your feet. The grace of our Lord Jesus Christ be with you.

—Romans 16:20

1 Corinthians

Therefore purge out the old yeast, that you may be a new batch, since you are unleavened. For even Christ, our Passover, has been sacrificed for us.

—1 Corinthians 5:7

But I say that the things which the Gentiles sacrifice, they sacrifice to demons, and not to God. I do not want you to have fellowship with demons.

—1 Corinthians 10:20

You cannot drink the cup of the Lord and the cup of demons. You cannot be partakers of the Lord's table and of the table of demons.

—1 Corinthians 10:21

2 Corinthians

He delivered us from so great a death and does deliver us. In Him we trust that He will still deliver us.

—2 Corinthians 1:10

...lest Satan should take advantage of us. For we are not ignorant of his devices.

—2 Corinthians 2:11

Now the Lord is the Spirit. And where the Spirit of the Lord is, there is liberty.

—2 Corinthians 3:17

For the weapons of our warfare are not carnal, but mighty through God to the pulling down of strongholds.

—2 Corinthians 10:4

And no wonder! For even Satan disguises himself as an angel of light.

—2 Corinthians 11:14

Galatians

Who gave Himself for our sins, that He might deliver us from this present evil age, according to the will of our God and Father.

—Galatians 1:4

Christ has redeemed us from the curse of the law by being made a curse for us—as it is written, "Cursed is everyone who hangs on a tree."

—Galatians 3:13

For freedom Christ freed us. Stand fast therefore and do not be entangled again with the yoke of bondage.

—Galatians 5:1

Ephesians

…which He performed in Christ when He raised Him from the dead and seated Him at His own right hand in the heavenly places, far above all principalities, and power, and might, and dominion, and every name that is named, not only in this age but also in that which is to come. And He put all things in subjection under His feet and made Him the head over all things for the church.

—Ephesians 1:20–22

Do not give place to the devil.

—Ephesians 4:27

Put on the whole armor of God that you may be able to stand against the schemes of the devil. For our fight is not against flesh and blood, but against principalities, against powers, against the rulers of the darkness of this world, and against spiritual forces of evil in the heavenly places. Therefore take up the whole armor of God that you may be able to resist in the evil day, and having done all, to stand.

—Ephesians 6:11–13

Colossians

He has delivered us from the power of darkness and has transferred us into the kingdom of His dear Son.

—Colossians 1:13

And having disarmed authorities and powers, He made a show of them openly, triumphing over them by the cross.

—Colossians 2:15

2 Thessalonians

And pray that we may be delivered from unreasonable and wicked men, for not all men have faith.

—2 Thessalonians 3:2

1 Timothy

He must not be newly converted, so that he does not become prideful and fall into the condemnation of the devil.

—1 Timothy 3:6

Moreover he must have a good reputation among those who are outsiders, so that he does not fall into reproach and the snare of the devil.

—1 TIMOTHY 3:7

Now the Spirit clearly says that in the last times some will depart from the faith and pay attention to seducing spirits and doctrines of devils.

—1 TIMOTHY 4:1

For some have already turned aside after Satan.

—1 TIMOTHY 5:15

2 Timothy

And they may escape from the snare of the devil, after being captured by him to do his will.

—2 TIMOTHY 2:26

But the Lord stood with me and strengthened me, so that through me the preaching might be fully known, and that all the Gentiles might hear. And I was delivered out of the mouth of the lion.

—2 TIMOTHY 4:17

Hebrews

So then, as the children share in flesh and blood, He likewise took part in these, so that through death He might destroy him who has the power of death, that is, the devil.

—HEBREWS 2:14

...and deliver those who through fear of death were throughout their lives subject to bondage.

—HEBREWS 2:15

By faith they passed through the Red Sea as on dry land, which the Egyptians attempted to do, but were drowned.

—HEBREWS 11:29

Make straight paths for your feet, lest that which is lame go out of joint, but rather be healed.

—HEBREWS 12:13

So we may boldly say: "The Lord is my helper; I will not fear. What can man do to me?"

—HEBREWS 13:6

James

You believe that there is one God; you do well. The demons also believe and tremble.

—JAMES 2:19

This wisdom descends not from above, but is earthly, unspiritual, and devilish.

—JAMES 3:15

For where there is envying and strife, there is confusion and every evil work.

—JAMES 3:16

Therefore submit yourselves to God. Resist the devil, and he will flee from you.

—JAMES 4:7

Confess your faults to one another and pray for one another, that you may be healed. The effective, fervent prayer of a righteous man accomplishes much.

—James 5:16

1 Peter

Be sober and watchful, because your adversary the devil walks around as a roaring lion, seeking whom he may devour. Resist him firmly in the faith, knowing that the same afflictions are experienced by your brotherhood throughout the world.

—1 Peter 5:8–9

2 Peter

And if He delivered righteous Lot, who was distressed by the filthy conduct of the wicked.

—2 Peter 2:7

Then the Lord knows how to rescue the godly from trial, and to keep the unrighteous under punishment for the Day of Judgment.

—2 Peter 2:9

1 John

Whoever practices sin is of the devil, for the devil has been sinning from the beginning. For this purpose the Son of God was revealed, that He might destroy the works of the devil.

—1 John 3:8

In this the children of God and the children of the devil are revealed: Whoever does not live in righteousness is not of God, nor is the one who does not love his brother.

—1 JOHN 3:10

There is no fear in love, but perfect love casts out fear, because fear has to do with punishment. Whoever fears is not perfect in love.

—1 JOHN 4:18

Revelation

And from Jesus Christ, who is the faithful witness, the firstborn from the dead, and the ruler of the kings of the earth. To Him who loved us and washed us from our sins in His own blood.

—REVELATION 1:5

He who has an ear, let him hear what the Spirit says to the churches. To him who overcomes I will give permission to eat of the tree of life, which is in the midst of the Paradise of God.

—REVELATION 2:7

To the angel of the church in Smyrna write: "The First and the Last, who was dead and came to life, says these things."

—REVELATION 2:8

He who has an ear, let him hear what the Spirit says to the churches. To him who overcomes I will give the hidden manna to eat. And I will give him a white stone, and on the stone a new name written, which no one knows except he who receives it.

—Revelation 2:17

To him who overcomes and keeps My works to the end, I will give authority over the nations—He "shall rule them with a rod of iron; like the vessels of a potter they shall be broken in pieces"—even as I myself have received authority from My Father. And I will give him the morning star.

—Revelation 2:26–28

He who overcomes shall be clothed in white garments. I will not blot his name out of the Book of Life, but I will confess his name before My Father and before His angels.

—Revelation 3:5

He who overcomes will I make a pillar in the temple of My God, and he shall go out no more. I will write on him the name of My God and the name of the city of My God, the New Jerusalem, which comes down out of heaven from My God, and My own new name.

—Revelation 3:12

They overcame him by the blood of the Lamb and by the word of their testimony, and they loved not their lives unto the death.

—Revelation 12:11

For they are spirits of demons, performing signs, who go out to the kings of the earth and of the whole world, to gather them to the battle of that great day of God Almighty.

—Revelation 16:14

These will wage war with the Lamb, but the Lamb will overcome them, for He is Lord of lords and King of kings. Those who are with Him are called and chosen and faithful.

—Revelation 17:14

He cried out mightily with a loud voice, saying: "'Fallen! Fallen is Babylon the Great!' She has become a dwelling place of demons, a haunt for every unclean spirit, and a haunt for every unclean and hateful bird."

—Revelation 18:2

Then I heard another voice from heaven saying: "'Come out of her, my people,' lest you partake in her sins, and lest you receive her plagues."

—Revelation 18:4

He is clothed with a robe dipped in blood. His name is called The Word of God.

—Revelation 19:13

They traveled the breadth of the earth and surrounded the camp of the saints and the beloved city. But fire came down from God out of heaven and devoured them. The devil, who deceived them, was cast into the lake of fire and brimstone where the beast and the false prophet were. They will be tormented day and night forever and ever.

—Revelation 20:9–10

...in the middle of its street. On each side of the river was the tree of life, which bore twelve kinds of fruit, yielding its fruit each month. The leaves of the tree were for the healing of the nations.

—Revelation 22:2

PART III

HEALING
SCRIPTURES

7

BY HIS STRIPES
YOU ARE HEALED

PHYSICAL, EMOTIONAL, AND SPIRITUAL HEALING are available to all who put their trust in God. It is amazing that some Christians still believe that God puts sickness on His people. Some may ask, "God, why do You allow this sickness to come upon my body?" They feel, or may have been told by a church leader, that it is the will of God for them to suffer sickness and not be healed. However, that is not biblical. God does not put sickness on His people. Jesus died so we can be healed. I do believe that there may be times when God allows sickness, especially for rebellion or disobedience. But for God's people we can expect to live in health and to be healed of all our diseases because of what Jesus did on the cross.

In this section of the book I have highlighted all the scriptures in the Bible that talk about healing. When we know what God says about healing, and because God is faithful to His word, we can have faith to believe His promises to heal. Supernatural healing is activated by faith. Without faith the miracle-working power of God becomes dormant in our lives. (See Matthew 13:58; Mark 6:5.) "Faith comes by hearing, and hearing by the word of God" (Rom. 10:17).

How Healing and Infirmity Are Expressed in the Bible

Written in Hebrew, Greek, and Aramaic, the Bible uses various words from those languages to reveal to us God's healing power. In Hebrew the word *rapha* found in Isaiah 53:5 is translated cure, make whole, heal, health, and physician.[1] The New Testament also uses the Hebrew words *marpe* (Mal. 4:2), translated as healing, health, cure, remedy, sound in health, and wholesome[2]; and *aruwkah*[3] (Jer. 8:22), which means restoration to sound health.

The New Testament uses the Greek word *therapeuo* (Luke 4:23–24), meaning heal.[4] It also uses the word *diasozo* (Matt. 14:36), whose root word is *sozo*.[5] We often relate the word *sozo* to salvation only, but when used as part of the word *diasozo*, it also means to heal thoroughly, make perfectly whole, and is used of the body being healed.[6] It's amazing that this word, commonly related to *save* or *salvation*, also includes healing and deliverance from sickness and infirmity.

The Hebrew word for *sick* is *choliy*, which means affliction, disease, grief, griefs, illness, sick, sickness, and sicknesses.[7]

When we are saved, we are saved wholly and completely, from the inside out, physically and spiritually, from the top of our heads to the soles of our feet, and this extends to all that concerns us.

Twelve Biblical Ways to Healing

The Bible demonstrates many ways that God brings healing to His people. We should not get caught up in one method of healing. God is all-powerful and all-knowing. His ways are not our ways. He works in both the seen and the unseen, the tested and the unproven. There are many ways you can expect God to heal you. The first place you start is with prayer and faith, and then His healing will come. The twelve ways I have listed here come from my studies, but do not put limits on God. He wants to heal you, and He will do it in His way and in His time.

1. Laying on of hands (Luke 4:40)

Healing virtue can flow through the laying on of hands. We see this demonstrated many times through Jesus's and the apostles' ministries.

2. Deliverance (Matt. 8:16)

Demons can be the reason people are sick in their bodies. They may have a spirit of infirmity. See also Luke 8:2.

3. Breaking generational curses (Gal. 3:13)

People are tormented by generational demonic spirits of infirmity that manifest as diabetes, high blood pressure, certain heart conditions, and more. If there is a generational curse that is causing sickness in your body, you will need to go through deliverance to have that demon cast out of your life. You have the authority through Christ to tell the devil that he will not put this sickness in your body. Tell him, "I don't care if my mother, grandmother, or great-grandmother had this disease; the curse stops here. I break it in the name of Jesus." Begin to rise up and use your authority! Say, "I am not cursed. I am blessed. My body is blessed with healing, in Jesus's name."

4. Anointing oil (Mark 6:13)

Anointing oil represents the Spirit of God and the anointing. The anointing is what drives sickness and disease out of our bodies. The anointing oil breaks yokes of bondage (Isa. 10:27), and sickness is a form of bondage.

5. Faith (Mark 11:23)

For some people sickness is a mountain. It's always in their way. It seems like something they can't overcome. But Mark 11:23 says when you have faith and don't doubt, you will speak to a mountain, and it will move. So speak to that mountain of sickness; don't climb it! You have to talk to mountains: "Lupus, be removed and cast in the sea!" "Cancer, be removed and cast in the sea!" But don't doubt in your heart. This is why you have to carefully guard your heart. Don't hang around people who doubt. Keep your heart free from doubt and unbelief.

There is going to come a time when you will have to

speak to some things. Every time a mountain gets in your way, instead of turning around and running, you need to stand face-to-face and say, "Be thou removed!" Grow up in faith. Open your mouth and talk to sickness. Say, "I command this sickness to leave my body in the name of Jesus." Mark 11:23 says, "…those things which he saith" (KJV). This is not even about prayer. This is just speaking. Some stuff you have to just speak to! "He shall have whatsoever he saith" (KJV).

6. Touch (Mark 5:29–30)

Luke 6:19 says, "The whole crowd tried to touch Him, for power went out from Him and healed them all." Worship is a way to touch God and experience His healing power. True worshippers know how to get in God's presence. "But the hour cometh, and now is, when the true worshippers shall worship the Father in spirit and in truth: for the Father seeketh such to worship him" (John 4:23, KJV). Is this your hour?

7. God's presence (Luke 5:17)

"The power of the Lord was present to heal them." Praise and worship are there to invite God's presence in so people will get healed. It is not a warm-up to the message.

8. Prayer (Matt. 21:22)

James 5:16 says we must confess our faults and pray for one another, that we may be healed. Sometimes healing doesn't come until you confess your faults and let somebody pray for you. Sometimes the key is humility.

9. Gift of healing (1 Cor. 12:9, 28)

When Jesus left the earth, He said we would do greater works than He did. He also said He would send a helper to instruct us and guide us in these greater works. The Holy Spirit came among men to indwell us, giving us supernatural ability to carry out the works of Christ. He accomplishes this by endowing us with various gifts that all work together to bring people into relationship with God. One of these gifts is the gift of healing.

> God has put these in the church: first apostles, second prophets, third teachers, after that miracles, then gifts of healings, helps, governments, and various tongues.
>
> —1 Corinthians 12:28

10. Fasting (Isa. 58:8)

When you fast in the way that God leads you, He says that "your light shall break forth like the morning, your healing shall spring forth speedily, and your righteousness shall go before you; the glory of the Lord shall be your rear guard" (NKJV). According to this verse, you will be healed when you fast, but better yet fasting can serve as preventive medicine. It says, "The Lord shall be your rear guard." In other words, sickness can't sneak up on you. God's got your back. While everyone else is getting the swine flu, you're healthy. While there's no cure for the common cold, you sail through cold season with not so much as one symptom, sniffle, or cough.

Then there are just those times when nothing else will do except a sacrifice of going without food, a time to surrender your flesh to the Spirit of God that brings life. Jesus talks about this in Matthew 17:21 when He says, "This kind does not go out except by prayer and fasting."

11. God's prophetic word to you (Ps. 107:20)

The Bible says that God "sent His word and healed them and delivered them from their destruction" (Ps. 107:20). We also know that God's word does not return to Him void. It accomplishes everything it was sent to accomplish (Isa. 55:11). If He spoke healing to you, then you are healed. Jesus said that man would not live by bread alone but by every word that proceeds out of the mouth of God. That is why this book and others like it that help you with learning and meditating on the Word of God are so important for your healing. Declare, by the Word of God, "I shall not die, but I shall live and declare the works of the LORD" (Ps. 118:17). Read the Word. Confess the Word. Use the healing scriptures in this book. Trust God because His word will accomplish in you all the purposes for which it was sent.

12. Healing cloths/clothing (Acts 19:12)

The healing anointing is transferable. It can be in clothing. It is tangible. We pray over prayer cloths at my church, and people have been healed. Years ago while preaching in Ethiopia, I took my shirt off after ministering and cut it up into small pieces of cloth. We passed them out to all the people there, and we heard so many testimonies of healings. One person set a cloth on fire in his sick mother's home, and the smoke from the cloth healed her. She had been bedridden for years, and she got up out of her bed healed. In other countries they don't have doctors and hospitals as we do in America. They have to believe God. They are desperate for healing. They don't have all the prescription medicines, health insurance, Medicaid, and Medicare. So they come to services believing that if they don't get their healing there, they are not going to make it. They have high expectancy and high faith. God honors faith.

> And when the men of that place recognized Him, they sent word to all the surrounding country and brought to Him all who were sick, and begged Him that they might only touch the hem of His garment. And as many as touched it were made perfectly well.
> —Matthew 14:35–36

> God worked powerful miracles by the hands of Paul. So handkerchiefs or aprons he had touched were brought to the sick, and the diseases left them, and the evil spirits went out of them.
> —Acts 19:11–12

Now that you've seen how healing is expressed throughout the Bible, let's look at all the verses in the Bible that you can claim for receiving healing or the healing anointing to pray for healing for others.

8

HEALING IN THE
OLD TESTAMENT

IN THE OLD TESTAMENT, God revealed His healing
power through prophets such as Moses, Elijah, and
Elisha. He also brought healing to people directly Himself. We see examples of God's miraculous healing power
in the lives of Sarah (Gen. 18:10, 14; 21:1–3), Abimelech
(Gen. 20:1–8), Moses's sister and prophetess Miriam
(Num. 12:1–15), Manoah's wife (Judg. 13:2–25), Hannah
(1 Sam. 1:5, 19–20), King Jeroboam (1 Kings 13:4–6), the
widow's son in 1 Kings 17:17–24, the Shunammite woman
(2 Kings 4:8–17), Naaman (2 Kings 5:1–14), King Hezekiah (2 Kings 20:1–7; 2 Chron. 32:24–26; Isa. 38:1–8),
Job (Job 42:10–17), and King Nebuchadnezzar (Dan. 4:34,
36), and then there are mass and corporate healings found
in Numbers 16:46–50; 21:4–9; 2 Samuel 24:10–25.[1]

When we get to the Book of Isaiah, we see a prophetic foreshadowing of the healing ministry of Christ.
The prophet Isaiah reveals that Jesus bore our griefs and

sorrows (Isa. 53:4). What causes so much grief and so much sorrow? Sickness and disease. When you're not healthy, you can't enjoy the blessings and the fullness of God. Isaiah 53 is the redemptive chapter. Verse 5 talks about being healed by the stripes of Jesus. The Bible says Jesus took thirty-nine lashes on His back and body. There are thirty-nine major types of sickness and disease. Every stripe that Jesus endured took care of a different sickness and disease.

Young's Literal Translation translates Isaiah 53:4 this way: "Surely our sicknesses he hath borne, and *our pains*— he hath carried them" (emphasis added). Not even our pain is acceptable to the Lord. He wants us to be healed even from the symptoms of physical ailments. Millions of dollars are spent on pain relief. Toothaches, headaches, neck pain, earaches, joint pain, back pain—and Jesus will heal you from it all. Let's look at how.

Genesis

But God came to Abimelek in a dream by night and said to him, "You are a dead man because of the woman whom you have taken, for she is a man's wife."

Abimelek had not gone near her, and he said, "Lord, will You slay a righteous nation? Did he not say to me, 'She is my sister,' and did not even she herself say, 'He is my brother'? In the integrity of my heart and innocence of my hands I have done this."

And God said to him in a dream, "Yes, I know

that you did this in the integrity of your heart. For I also kept you from sinning against Me. Therefore, I did not let you touch her. Therefore return the man's wife, for he is a prophet and he will pray for you. Moreover, you will live. However, if you do not return her, know that you will surely die, you and all who are yours."

—Genesis 20:3–7

Exodus

The blood shall be to you for a sign on the houses where you are. And when I see the blood, I will pass over you, and the plague shall not be upon you to destroy you when I smite the land of Egypt.

—Exodus 12:13

He said, "If you diligently listen to the voice of the Lord your God, and do what is right in His sight, and give ear to His commandments, and keep all His statutes, I will not afflict you with any of the diseases with which I have afflicted the Egyptians. For I am the Lord who heals you."

—Exodus 15:26

If he gets up and walks around on his staff, then he who struck him shall go unpunished. Only he must pay for his loss of time and shall see to it that he is thoroughly healed.

—Exodus 21:19

You shall serve the Lord your God, and He shall bless your bread and your water, and I will remove sickness from your midst.

—Exodus 23:25

Leviticus

If you continue to walk contrary to Me and will not listen to Me, I will bring seven times more plagues upon you according to your sins.

—Leviticus 26:21

Numbers

And Moses cried out to the Lord, saying, "O God, heal her, I pray!"

—Numbers 12:13

Deuteronomy

The Lord will take away from you all sickness, and will afflict you with none of the evil diseases of Egypt, which you know, but will lay them on all those who hate you.

—Deuteronomy 7:15

If you are not careful to observe all the words of this law that are written in this book so that you may fear this glorious and fearful name, the Lord your God, then the Lord will bring extraordinary plagues on you and your descendants, even great long-lasting plagues, and severe and long-lasting sicknesses. Moreover, He will bring all the diseases of Egypt upon you, which you were afraid of, and they will cling to you. Also every sickness and every plague which is not written in the Book of the Law will the Lord bring upon you until you are destroyed.

—Deuteronomy 28:58–61

See now that I, even I, am He, and there is no god besides Me; I kill, and I make alive; I wound, and I heal; there is no one who can deliver out of My hand.

—Deuteronomy 32:39

Moses was a hundred and twenty years old when he died. His eye was not dim, nor was his vitality diminished.

—Deuteronomy 34:7

2 Kings

Ahaziah fell down through a lattice in his upper chamber that was in Samaria and became ill. So he sent messengers and said to them, "Go, inquire of Baal-Zebub the god of Ekron whether I will recover from this illness."

But the angel of the Lord said to Elijah the Tishbite, "Arise, go up to meet the messengers of the king of Samaria, and say to them, 'Is it because there is not a God in Israel, that you go to inquire of Baal-Zebub the god of Ekron?' Therefore thus says the Lord, 'You will not come down from the bed on which you have gone up but will surely die.'" Then Elijah departed.

—2 Kings 1:2–4

He went out to the spring of water and threw the salt into it and said, "Thus says the Lord: I have healed this water. No more death or unfruitfulness will come from it."

—2 Kings 2:21

Turn back and say to Hezekiah the leader of My people: Thus says the Lord, the God of David your father: I have heard your prayer; I have seen your tears. I will heal you. On the third day you shall go up to the house of the Lord.

—2 Kings 20:5

2 Chronicles

If My people, who are called by My name, will humble themselves and pray, and seek My face and turn from their wicked ways, then I will hear from heaven, and will forgive their sin and will heal their land.

—2 Chronicles 7:14

In the thirty-ninth year of the reign of Asa, he had a sickness in his feet until his sickness became grave. Even in his disease he did not seek after the Lord, but the physicians.

—2 Chronicles 16:12

So the Lord heard Hezekiah and healed the people.

—2 Chronicles 30:20

But they continued to jest regarding the messengers of God, despising His word and making fun of

His prophets until the wrath of the Lord came up against His people, until there was no remedy.

—2 Chronicles 36:16

Job

For He inflicts pain, but He binds up and gives relief; He wounds, but His hands also heal.

—Job 5:18, amp

He keeps back his soul from the pit, and his life from perishing by the sword.

He is also chastened with pain on his bed, and with strong pain in many of his bones, so that his life abhors bread, and his soul dainty food. His flesh is consumed away that it cannot be seen, and his bones that were not seen stick out. Yes, his soul draws near to the grave, and his life to the executioners.

If there is a messenger for him, an interpreter, one among a thousand, to show to man what is right for him, then He is gracious to him, and says, "Deliver him from going down to the pit; I have found a ransom." His flesh will be fresher than a child's; he will return to the days of his youth; he will pray to God, and He will be favorable unto him, and he will see His face with joy, for He will render unto man His righteousness.

—Job 33:18–26

Psalms

Be gracious to me, O Lord, for I am weak; O Lord, heal me, for my bones are terrified.

—Psalm 6:2

For You will save the afflicted people, but will bring down prideful eyes.

—Psalm 18:27

For He has not despised nor abhorred the affliction of the afflicted; nor has He hid His face from him; but when he cried to Him, He heard.

—Psalm 22:24

Turn to me, and be gracious to me, for I am isolated and afflicted.

—Psalm 25:16

Look on my pain and misery, and forgive all my sins.

—Psalm 25:18

I had fainted, unless I had believed to see the goodness of the Lord in the land of the living.

—Psalm 27:13, kjv

O Lord my God, I cried to You, and You healed me.

—Psalm 30:2

But as for me, when they were sick, my clothing was sackcloth; I humbled my soul with fasting; and my prayer returns to my own heart.

—Psalm 35:13

O LORD, do not rebuke me in Your wrath, nor chasten me in Your hot displeasure. For Your arrows pierce me, and Your hand presses down on me. There is no soundness in my flesh because of Your indignation, nor is there health in my bones because of my sin.

For my iniquities have passed over my head; as a heavy burden they are too heavy for me. My wounds grow foul and fester because of my foolishness. I am bent, I am bowed down greatly; I go mourning all the day long. For my sides are filled with burning, and there is no soundness in my flesh.

I am numb and completely crushed; I have roared because of the groaning of my heart. Lord, all my desire is before You, and my sighing is not hidden from You. My heart throbs, my strength fails me; as for the light of my eyes, it also is gone from me.

My friends and my companions stand back because of my affliction, and those close to me stand at a distance. The people who seek my life strike at me; those who seek my harm speak destruction, and plan treacheries all the day long. But I, like a deaf man, did not hear; and like a dumb man, did not open my mouth. Thus I was as a man who does not hear, and in whose mouth are no reproofs.

For in You, O LORD, do I hope; You will answer, O Lord my God. For I said, "Lest otherwise they should rejoice over me. When my foot slips, they magnify themselves against me." For I am ready to stumble, and my pain is continually before me. For I will declare my iniquity; I am anxious because of my sin.

But my enemies are lively, and they are strong; and those who wrongfully hate me are many. Those also who repay evil for good are my adversaries, because I pursue good. Do not abandon me, O Lord; O my God, do not be far from me. Make haste to help me, O Lord, my salvation.

—Psalm 38:1–22

Blessed are those who consider the poor; the Lord will deliver them in the day of trouble. The Lord will preserve them and keep them alive, and they will be blessed on the earth, and You will not deliver them to the will of their enemies. The Lord will sustain them on the sickbed; You will restore all his lying down in his illness.

I said, "Lord, be gracious to me; heal my soul, for I have sinned against You."

—Psalm 41:1–4

Why, my soul, are you cast down? Why do you groan within me? Wait for God; I will yet thank Him, for He is my deliverance and my God.

—Psalm 42:11

Why are you cast down, O my soul? And why are you disquieted within me? Hope in God; for I will yet give Him thanks, the salvation of my countenance and my God.

—Psalm 43:5

Give ear to my prayer, O God, and do not hide Yourself from my supplication. Attend to me, and answer me; I am restless in my complaint, and I murmur, because of the voice of the enemy, because of the pressure of the wicked, for they cause trouble to drop on me, and in wrath they have animosity against me.

My heart is in pain within me, and the terrors of death have fallen on me. Fear and trembling come into me, and horror has overwhelmed me.

I said, "Oh, that I had wings like a dove! For then I would fly away and be at rest. Indeed, then I would wander far off, and remain in the wilderness."

—PSALM 55:1–7

For You have delivered my soul from death, even my feet from stumbling, to walk before God in the light of the living.

—PSALM 56:13

You have made the earth tremble; You have split it open; heal its breaches, for it shook.

—PSALM 60:2

That Your way may be known on earth, Your salvation among all nations.

—PSALM 67:2

The enemy shall not take tribute from him, nor the wicked humiliate him.

—PSALM 89:22

There shall be no evil befall you, neither shall any plague come near your tent.

—Psalm 91:10

He shall call upon Me, and I will answer him; I will be with him in trouble, and I will deliver him and honor him. With long life I will satisfy him and show him My salvation.

—Psalm 91:15–16

…who forgives all your iniquities, who heals all your diseases.

—Psalm 103:3

Then He brought them out with silver and gold, and no one among their tribes faltered.

—Psalm 105:37

…and brought his people safely out from Egypt, loaded with silver and gold; there were no sick and feeble folk among them then.

—Psalm 105:37, tlb

He sent His word and healed them and delivered them from their destruction.

—Psalm 107:20

I love the Lord, because He has heard my voice and my supplications. Because He has inclined His ear to me, therefore I will call upon Him as long as I live. The cords of death encircled me, and the pains of Sheol took hold of me; I found trouble and sorrow.

Then called I upon the name of the Lord: "O Lord, I plead with You, deliver my soul."

Gracious is the LORD, and righteous; indeed, our God is merciful. The LORD protects the simple; I was brought low, and He helped me. Return to your rest, O my soul; for the LORD has vindicated you. For You have delivered my soul from death, my eyes from tears, and my feet from falling. I will walk before the LORD in the land of the living.

—PSALM 116:1–9

I shall not die, but I shall live and declare the works of the LORD.

—PSALM 118:17

Deal kindly with Your servant, that I may live and keep Your word.

—PSALM 119:17

I am greatly afflicted; revive me, O LORD, according to Your word.

—PSALM 119:107

I cried unto You, O LORD; I said, "You are my refuge and my portion in the land of the living."

—PSALM 142:5

He heals the broken in heart, and binds up their wounds.

—PSALM 147:3

Proverbs

It will be health to your body, and strength to your bones.

—PROVERBS 3:8

It will be health to your body [your marrow, your nerves, your sinews, your muscles—all your inner parts] and refreshment (physical well-being) to your bones.

—Proverbs 3:8, amp

...for they are life to those who find them, and health to all their body.

—Proverbs 4:22

For life they [are] to those finding them, And to all their flesh healing.

—Proverbs 4:22, ylt

Therefore his calamity will come suddenly; in a moment he will be broken without remedy.

—Proverbs 6:15

There is one who speaks like the piercings of a sword, but the tongue of the wise is health.

—Proverbs 12:18

Hope deferred makes the heart sick, but when the desire comes, it is a tree of life.

—Proverbs 13:12

A wicked messenger falls into mischief, but a faithful envoy is health.

—Proverbs 13:17

A sound heart is the life of the flesh, but envy the rottenness of the bones.

—Proverbs 14:30

The light of the eyes rejoices the heart, and a good report makes the bones healthy.

—Proverbs 15:30

A merry heart does good like a medicine, but a broken spirit dries the bones.

—Proverbs 17:22

Pleasant words are as a honeycomb, sweet to the soul and health to the bones.

—Proverbs 16:24

He who is often reproved, yet hardens his neck, will suddenly be destroyed, and that without remedy.

—Proverbs 29:1

Ecclesiastes

…a time to kill, and a time to heal; a time to break down, and a time to build up.

—Ecclesiastes 3:3

Isaiah

Make the heart of this people dull, and their ears heavy, and shut their eyes; lest they see with their eyes, and hear with their ears, and understand with their heart, and turn and be healed.

—Isaiah 6:10

Moreover the light of the moon shall be as the light of the sun, and the light of the sun shall be seven-fold, as the light of seven days, in the day that the

Lord binds up the breach of His people and heals the wound from His blow.

—Isaiah 30:26

In those days Hezekiah was mortally ill. And Isaiah the prophet, the son of Amoz, came to him and said to him, "Thus says the Lord: Set your house in order, for you shall die, and not live."

Then Hezekiah turned his face toward the wall, and prayed to the Lord, and said, "Remember now, O Lord, I beseech You, how I have walked before You in truth and with a perfect heart, and have done what is good in Your sight." And Hezekiah wept bitterly.

Then the word of the Lord came to Isaiah, saying: "Go, and say to Hezekiah, Thus says the Lord, the God of David your father: I have heard your prayer, I have seen your tears. Surely I will add to your days fifteen years."

—Isaiah 38:1–5

O Lord, by these things men live, and in all these is the life of my spirit; restore me to health and let me live!

—Isaiah 38:16, AMP

Surely he has borne our grief and carried our sorrows; yet we esteemed him stricken, smitten of God, and afflicted.

—Isaiah 53:4

Verily he suffered our sicknesses, and he bare our sorrows; and we areckoned him as a mesel, and smitten of God, and made low. (Truly he suffered our sicknesses, and he carried our sorrows; but we reckoned him like a leper, and struck by God, and abased, or made low.)

—ISAIAH 53:4, WYC

But [in fact] He has borne our griefs, and He has carried our sorrows and pains; yet we [ignorantly] assumed that He was stricken, struck down by God and degraded and humiliated [by Him].

—ISAIAH 53:4, AMP

But he was wounded for our transgressions, he was bruised for our iniquities; the chastisement of our peace was upon him, and by his stripes we are healed.

—ISAIAH 53:5

I have seen his ways but will heal him; I will lead him and restore comfort to him and to his mourners, by creating the fruit of the lips. Peace, peace to him who is far off and to him who is near, says the LORD, and I will heal him.

—ISAIAH 57:18–19

Then your light shall break forth as the morning, and your healing shall spring forth quickly, and your righteousness shall go before you; the glory of the LORD shall be your reward.

—ISAIAH 58:8

Jeremiah

Return, O backsliding sons, and I will heal your backslidings. "We come to You; for You are the LORD our God."

—Jeremiah 3:22

They have healed also the brokenness of the daughter of My people superficially, saying, "Peace, peace," when there is no peace.

—Jeremiah 6:14

For they have healed the brokenness of the daughter of My people superficially, saying, "Peace, peace," when there is no peace.

—Jeremiah 8:11

We looked for peace, but no good came; and for a time of health, but there was trouble!

—Jeremiah 8:15

Is there no balm in Gilead? Is there no physician there? Why then has not the health of the daughter of my people recovered?

—Jeremiah 8:22

Whether resin, that is, a gum of great odour and medicinal, is not in Gilead, either a leech is not there? Why therefore the wound of the daughter of my people is not healed perfectly? (Is there not resin, that is, a medicinal gum of strong odour, in Gilead, or is a physician not there? And so why is

the wound of the daughter of my people not perfectly healed?)

—JEREMIAH 8:22, WYC

Have You utterly rejected Judah? Has Your soul
loathed Zion? Why have You stricken us so that
there is no healing for us? We looked for peace, but
there was nothing good; and for the time of healing,
but there is trouble!

—JEREMIAH 14:19

Why is my pain perpetual and my wound incurable,
which refuses to be healed? Shall You be altogether
to me as a deceptive stream and as waters that fail?

—JEREMIAH 15:18

Heal me, O LORD, and I will be healed; save me,
and I will be saved, for You are my praise.

—JEREMIAH 17:14

There is no one to plead your cause that you may be
bound up. You have no healing medicines.

—JEREMIAH 30:13

For I will restore health to you, and I will heal you
of your wounds, says the LORD, because they called
you an outcast, saying, "This is Zion whom no man
cares for."

—JEREMIAH 30:17

I will bring it health and healing, and I will heal
them; and I will reveal to them the abundance of
peace and truth.

—JEREMIAH 33:6

Ezekiel

The diseased you have not strengthened, nor have you healed that which was sick, nor have you bound up that which was broken, nor have you brought back that which was driven away, nor have you sought that which was lost. But with force and with cruelty you have subjugated them.

—Ezekiel 34:4

Then he said to me, "This water flows toward the eastern region and goes down into the valley, and enters the sea. When it flows into the sea, the water will become fresh."

—Ezekiel 47:8

Every living creature that swarms, wherever the rivers go, will live. And there shall be a very great multitude of fish, because these waters shall come there and the others become fresh. Thus everything shall live wherever the river comes.

—Ezekiel 47:9

But its miry places and its marshes shall not be healed. They shall be given to salt. By the river upon its bank, on this side and on that side, shall grow all kinds of trees for food, whose leaf shall not fade nor shall its fruit fail. They shall bring forth fruit according to their months, because their water issues out of the sanctuary. And their fruit shall be for food and their leaves for medicine.

—Ezekiel 47:11–12

Joel

And I will compensate you for the years the locusts have eaten—the larval locust, the hopper locust, and the fledging locust—My great army which I sent against you.

—Joel 2:25

Malachi

But for you who fear My name, the sun of righteousness will rise with healing in its wings. You will go out and grow up like calves from the stall.

—Malachi 4:2

9

HEALING IN THE NEW TESTAMENT

IN THE NEW TESTAMENT we are no longer dealing in types and shadows. Jesus's coming to the earth signified the fulfillment of God's covenant with man. He restored our ability to go to God directly for all we need. We do not need to go to the prophet, the king, or any leader to receive what we need from God. The one thing we must do first is accept Jesus's sacrifice on the cross by faith and know that we are forgiven. Our right to the covenant promises has been restored once and for all.

Along with fulfilling the covenant, Jesus also came to demonstrate God's loving-kindness to mankind. He came to show the true nature of the Spirit of God. He came to show that where the Father's presence and glory dwell, no sin or sickness can exist in the same place. With the Spirit of God dwelling in us, we no longer have to put up with the oppression of the enemy in any of its forms, including sickness and disease. This is what we find when we read the New Testament. We should read it as revealing the Spirit of God in light of a new covenant that He has made with man. And with that new covenant comes healing of all our diseases.

Healing Accompanies the Message of the Kingdom

Wherever Jesus preached the message of the kingdom, people were healed. Jesus introduced a whole new age—the kingdom age. Because of this we don't have to be sick, broke, or run over by the devil any longer. This is good news Jesus came to bring! This is what the New Testament and the new covenant are all about. You don't have to be sick, broke, poor, or confused any longer. Sickness and disease are works of the devil, and Jesus came and "disarmed authorities and powers, He made a show of them openly, triumphing over them by the cross" (Col. 2:15).

Healing comes with the territory. When you are in covenant with God through faith in Christ, you can expect to be healed. Mark 16:17–18 says, "These signs will accompany those who believe: In My name they will cast out demons; they will speak with new tongues; they will take up serpents; if they drink any deadly thing, it will not hurt them; they will lay hands on the sick, and they will recover." So as a citizen of the kingdom not only should you expect to be healed, but you should also know that you are commissioned to heal those around you. This is true kingdom living.

There Isn't One Sickness or Disease Jesus Can't Heal

Physical illness can be one of the worst things that can happen to an individual, and as we read in the Old Testament, Jesus had become acquainted with our sorrows and pain. The compassion that drives Him to heal us comes from His being acquainted with what we suffer as humans. Jesus cares about people. He had no problem breaking man-made religious laws and traditions to see people healed. He had great compassion on the people who came to Him. He wasn't going to let the Pharisees or any judgmental leaders of His day or of ours come between people and their healing.

In Matthew 9:36 the Bible says that "when [Jesus] saw the multitudes, He was moved with compassion for them, because they were weary and scattered, like sheep having no shepherd." It is not God's plan for you to hurt and suffer. The New Testament scriptures reveal His plan for you to be set free from every sickness, ailment, illness, dysfunction, and disease.

The following scriptures will show that when Jesus walked the earth, there was nothing that He didn't heal. When He left, He sent the Holy Spirit, who works in us to experience the fullness of salvation Jesus delivered to us on the cross. Again, reading these verses will help you have confidence that what was good for the people then is good for us now. You will have faith to believe that Jesus is the same yesterday, today, and forever (Heb. 13:8). God does not change (Mal. 3:6). There is no shadow of turning with Him (James 1:17). Because of God's faithfulness you can trust that if He healed then, He will heal today.

Matthew 4:23 says, "Jesus went throughout all Galilee teaching in their synagogues, preaching the gospel of the kingdom, and healing *all kinds of sickness and all sorts of diseases* among the people" (emphasis added). Jesus healed every person who came to Him with a disease or sickness— no exceptions. There is nothing too hard for Him. Don't let the devil or the doctor tell you that you have something that's incurable. It might be incurable to the doctor, but it's not incurable to God.

> When evening had come, they brought to Him
> many who were demon-possessed. And He cast out
> the spirits with a word, and healed all who were sick.
> —MATTHEW 8:16, NKJV

Jesus's healing ministry was just the beginning. He commissioned the disciples to do even greater works than He did:

> Truly, truly I say to you, he who believes in Me will
> do the works that I do also. And he will do greater
> works than these, because I am going to My Father.
> —JOHN 14:12

The following scriptures for healing will start with the ministry of Christ and follow through to what His disciples did through the power of the Holy Spirit, and then move on to what you and I have been called and anointed to do. These scriptures build great faith to see healing come to your life and the lives of those to whom you minister.

Matthew

Jesus went throughout all Galilee teaching in their synagogues, preaching the gospel of the kingdom, and healing all kinds of sickness and all sorts of diseases among the people.

—MATTHEW 4:23

His fame went throughout all Syria. And they brought to Him all sick people who were taken with various diseases and tormented with pain, those who were possessed with demons, those who had seizures, and those who had paralysis, and He healed them.

—MATTHEW 4:24

And then a leper came and worshipped Him, saying, "Lord, if You are willing, You can make me clean." Jesus reached out His hand and touched him, saying, "I will. Be clean." And immediately his leprosy was cleansed.

—MATTHEW 8:2–3

Jesus said to him, "I will come and heal him."

—MATTHEW 8:7

The centurion answered and said, "Lord, I am not worthy that You should come under my roof. But speak the word only, and my servant will be healed."

—MATTHEW 8:8

Then Jesus said to the centurion, "Go your way. And as you have believed, so let it be done for you." And his servant was healed that very moment.

—Matthew 8:13

When the evening came, they brought to Him many who were possessed with demons. And He cast out the spirits with His word, and healed all who were sick, to fulfill what was spoken by Isaiah the prophet, "He Himself took our infirmities and bore our sicknesses."

—Matthew 8:16–17

They brought to Him a man sick with paralysis, lying on a bed. And Jesus, seeing their faith, said to the paralytic, "Son, be of good cheer. Your sins are forgiven you."

—Matthew 9:2

"...But that you may know that the Son of Man has authority on earth to forgive sins"—then He said to the paralytic, "Arise, pick up your bed, and go into your house."

—Matthew 9:6

But when Jesus heard that, He said to them, "Those who are well do not need a physician, but those who are sick."

—Matthew 9:12

But Jesus turned around, and when He saw her, He said, "Daughter, be of good comfort. Your faith has made you well." And the woman was made well instantly.

—MATTHEW 9:22

Jesus went throughout all the cities and villages, teaching in their synagogues, preaching the gospel of the kingdom, and healing every sickness and every disease among the people.

—MATTHEW 9:35

He called His twelve disciples to Him and gave them authority over unclean spirits, to cast them out, and to heal all kinds of sickness and all kinds of disease.

—MATTHEW 10:1

Heal the sick, cleanse the lepers, raise the dead, and cast out demons. Freely you have received, freely give.

—MATTHEW 10:8

Jesus answered them, "Go and tell John what you hear and see: The blind receive their sight and the lame walk, the lepers are cleansed and the deaf hear, the dead are raised up, and the poor have the gospel preached to them. Blessed is he who does not fall away because of Me."

—MATTHEW 11:4–6

And there was a man whose hand had withered. They asked Him, "Is it lawful to heal on the Sabbath?" that they might accuse Him.

—MATTHEW 12:10

But when Jesus knew it, He withdrew from there. And great crowds followed Him, and He healed them all.

—Matthew 12:15

Then one possessed with a demon was brought to Him, blind and mute, and He healed him, so that the blind and mute man both spoke and saw.

—Matthew 12:22

For this people's heart has grown dull. Their ears have become hard of hearing, and they have closed their eyes, lest they should see with their eyes and hear with their ears and understand with their hearts, and turn, and I should heal them.

—Matthew 13:15

Jesus went ashore and saw a great assembly. And He was moved with compassion toward them, and He healed their sick.

—Matthew 14:14

And when the men of that place recognized Him, they sent word to all the surrounding country and brought to Him all who were sick, and begged Him that they might only touch the hem of His garment. And as many as touched it were made perfectly well.

—Matthew 14:35–36

Then Jesus answered her, "O woman, great is your faith. Let it be done for you as you desire." And her daughter was healed instantly.

—Matthew 15:28

Great crowds came to Him, having with them those who were lame, blind, mute, maimed, and many others, and placed them down at Jesus' feet, and He healed them.

—MATTHEW 15:30

Jesus rebuked the demon, and he came out of him. And the child was healed instantly.

—MATTHEW 17:18

Jesus said to them, "Because of your unbelief. For truly I say to you, if you have faith as a grain of mustard seed, you will say to this mountain, 'Move from here to there,' and it will move. And nothing will be impossible for you."

—MATTHEW 17:20

Large crowds followed Him, and He healed them there.

—MATTHEW 19:2

But Jesus looked at them and said, "With men this is impossible, but with God all things are possible."

—MATTHEW 19:26

There, two blind men sitting by the road, when they heard that Jesus was passing by, cried out, "Have mercy on us, O Lord, Son of David!" The crowd rebuked them, that they should be silent. But they cried out even more, "Have mercy on us, O Lord, Son of David!" Jesus stood still and called them, saying, "What do you want Me to do for you?" They said to Him, "Lord, let our eyes be opened." So Jesus had compassion on them and touched their eyes. Immediately their eyes received sight, and they followed Him.

—Matthew 20:30–34

The blind and the lame came to Him in the temple, and He healed them.

—Matthew 21:14

Mark

The mother of Simon's wife lay sick with a fever, and immediately they told Him of her. So He came and took her by the hand and lifted her up, and immediately the fever left her. And she served them. In the evening, when the sun had set, they brought to Him all who were sick and those who were possessed with demons. The whole city was gathered at the door, and He healed many who were sick with various diseases and cast out many demons.

—Mark 1:30–34

When they could not come near Him due to the crowding, they uncovered the roof where He was. When they had broken it open, they let down the bed on which the paralytic lay. When Jesus saw their faith, He said to the paralytic, "Son, your sins are forgiven you."

—Mark 2:4–5

They watched Him to see whether He would heal him on the Sabbath, so that they might accuse Him.

—Mark 3:2

For He had healed many, so that all who had diseases pressed on Him to touch Him.

—Mark 3:10

...and to have authority to heal sicknesses and to cast out demons...

—Mark 3:15

One of the rulers of the synagogue...earnestly asked Him, "My little daughter is lying at the point of death. I ask You, come and lay Your hands on her, so that she may be healed. And she will live."

—Mark 5:23

And a certain woman had a hemorrhage for twelve years, and had suffered much under many physicians. She had spent all that she had, and was not better but rather grew worse. When she had heard of Jesus, she came in the crowd behind Him and touched His garment. For she said, "If I may touch His garments, I shall be healed." And immediately her hemorrhage dried up, and she felt in her body that she was healed of the affliction.

—Mark 5:25–29

He could not do any miracles there, except that He laid His hands on a few sick people and healed them.

—Mark 6:5

And they cast out many demons and anointed with oil many who were sick and healed them.

—Mark 6:13

When they had come out of the boat, immediately
the people recognized Him, and ran throughout the
surrounding region, and began to carry the sick on
beds to wherever they heard He was. And wherever
He entered, into villages, cities, or the country, they
laid the sick in the marketplaces and pleaded with
Him that they might touch even the fringe of His
garment. And as many as touched Him were healed.

—Mark 6:54–56

Jesus, looking at them, said, "With men it is impossible, but not with God. For with God all things
are possible."

—Mark 10:27

For truly I say to you, whoever says to this mountain, "Be removed and be thrown into the sea," and
does not doubt in his heart, but believes that what
he says will come to pass, he will have whatever he
says. Therefore I say to you, whatever things you ask
when you pray, believe that you will receive them,
and you will have them.

—Mark 11:23–24

They will take up serpents; if they drink any deadly
thing, it will not hurt them; they will lay hands on
the sick, and they will recover.

—Mark 16:18

Luke

For with God nothing will be impossible.

—Luke 1:37

The Spirit of the Lord is upon Me, because He has anointed Me to preach the gospel to the poor; He has sent Me to heal the broken-hearted, to preach deliverance to the captives and recovery of sight to the blind, to set at liberty those who are oppressed.

—Luke 4:18

He said to them, "You will surely say to Me this proverb, 'Physician, heal Yourself. Whatever we have heard done in Capernaum, do also here in Your country.'"

—Luke 4:23

Now when the sun was setting, all those who had anyone sick with various diseases brought them to Him. And He laid His hands on every one of them and healed them.

—Luke 4:40

Yet even more so His fame went everywhere. And great crowds came together to hear and to be healed by Him of their infirmities.

—Luke 5:15

On a certain day, as He was teaching, Pharisees and teachers of the law were sitting nearby, who had come from every town of Galilee and Judea and from Jerusalem. And the power of the Lord was present to heal the sick.

—Luke 5:17

The scribes and the Pharisees watched Him to see whether He would heal on the Sabbath, so that they might find an accusation against Him.

—Luke 6:7

He came down with them and stood on a level place with a crowd of His disciples and a great crowd of people from all Judea and Jerusalem, and from the seacoast of Tyre and Sidon, who came to hear Him and be healed of their diseases, including those who were vexed by unclean spirits. And they were healed.

—Luke 6:17–18

The whole crowd tried to touch Him, for power went out from Him and healed them all.

—Luke 6:19

When he heard of Jesus, he sent the elders of the Jews to Him, asking Him to come and heal his servant.

—Luke 7:3

Likewise, I did not think myself worthy to come to You. But say the word, and my servant will be healed.

—Luke 7:7

When He came near the gate of the city, a man who had died was being carried out, the only son of his mother, and she was a widow. And a large crowd from the city was with her. When the Lord saw her, He had compassion on her and said to her, "Do not weep." Then He came and touched the coffin, and those who carried it stood still. He said, "Young man, I say to you, arise." He who was dead sat up and began to speak. And He gave him to his mother.

—LUKE 7:12–15

In that same hour He cured many of their infirmities and afflictions and evil spirits. And to many who were blind He gave sight.

—LUKE 7:21

...and some women who had been healed of evil spirits and infirmities: Mary, called Magdalene, from whom seven demons had come out...

—LUKE 8:2

Those who had seen it told them how he who had been possessed by demons was healed.

—LUKE 8:36

And a woman having a hemorrhage for twelve years, who had spent all her living on physicians, but could not be healed by anyone, came behind Him, and touched the fringe of His garment. And immediately her hemorrhage dried up.

—LUKE 8:43–44

When the woman saw that she was not hidden, she came trembling. And falling down before Him, she declared to Him before all the people why she had touched Him and how she was healed immediately.

—LUKE 8:47

Then He called His twelve disciples together and gave them power and authority over all demons and to cure diseases. And He sent them to preach the kingdom of God and to heal the sick.

—Luke 9:1–2

So they departed and went through the towns, preaching the gospel and healing everywhere.

—Luke 9:6

But when the crowds knew it, they followed Him. And He welcomed them and spoke to them about the kingdom of God, and healed those who had need of healing.

—Luke 9:11

While he was coming, the demon threw him down and convulsed him. But Jesus rebuked the unclean spirit, and healed the child, and returned him to his father.

—Luke 9:42

Heal the sick who are there and say to them, "The kingdom of God has come near to you."

—Luke 10:9

…and went to him and bound up his wounds, pouring in oil and wine. Then he set him on his own donkey and brought him to an inn, and took care of him.

—Luke 10:34

And there was a woman who had a spirit of infirmity for eighteen years and was bent over and could not straighten herself up. When Jesus saw her, He called her and said to her, "Woman, you are loosed from your infirmity." Then He laid His hands on her, and immediately she was made straight and glorified God. But the ruler of the synagogue answered with indignation, because Jesus had healed on the Sabbath, and said to the people, "There are six days in which men ought to work. Therefore come and be healed on those days, but not on the Sabbath day."

—Luke 13:11–14

He said to them, "Go and tell that fox, 'Look, I cast out demons. And I perform healings today and tomorrow, and on the third day I shall be perfected.'"

—Luke 13:32

Jesus said to the lawyers and Pharisees, "Is it lawful to heal on the Sabbath?"

—Luke 14:3

But they remained silent. So He took him and healed him, and let him go.

—Luke 14:4

And it came to pass, as he went to Jerusalem, that he passed through the midst of Samaria and Galilee. And as he entered into a certain village, there met him ten men that were lepers, which stood afar off: and they lifted up their voices, and said, Jesus, Master, have mercy on us. And when he saw them, he said unto them, Go shew yourselves unto the priests. And it came to pass, that, as they went, they were cleansed. And one of them, when he saw that he was healed, turned back, and with a loud voice glorified God, and fell down on his face at his feet, giving him thanks: and he was a Samaritan. And Jesus answering said, Were there not ten cleansed? but where are the nine?

—Luke 17:11–17, kjv

He said, "What is impossible with men is possible with God."

—Luke 18:27

But Jesus said, "This is enough!" And He touched his ear and healed him.

—Luke 22:51

John

So Jesus came again to Cana of Galilee where He had made the water wine. And there was a certain nobleman whose son was sick in Capernaum. When he heard that Jesus had come out of Judea into Galilee, he went to Him, pleading that He would come down and heal his son, for he was at the point of death.

Then Jesus said to him, "Unless you see signs and wonders, you will not believe."

The nobleman said to Him, "Sir, come down before my child dies."

Jesus said to him, "Go your way. Your son lives."

And the man believed the word that Jesus spoke to him, and he went his way. While he was going down, his servants met him and told him, "Your son lives!" When he inquired of them the hour when he began to heal, they answered, "Yesterday at the seventh hour the fever left him."

—John 4:46–52

In these lay a great crowd of invalids, blind, lame, and paralyzed, waiting for the moving of the water. For an angel went down at a certain time into the pool and stirred up the water. After the stirring of the water, whoever stepped in first was healed of whatever disease he had. A certain man was there who had an illness for thirty-eight years. When Jesus saw him lying there, and knew that he had been in that condition now a long time, He said to him, "Do you want to be healed?"

The sick man answered Him, "Sir, I have no one to put me into the pool when the water is stirred. But while I am coming, another steps down before me."

Jesus said to him, "Rise, take up your bed and walk." Immediately the man was healed, took up his bed, and walked.

—John 5:3–9

The Jews therefore said to him who was cured, "It is the Sabbath day. It is not lawful for you to carry your bed."

—John 5:10

Now the man who was healed did not know who it was, for Jesus had withdrawn, as there was a crowd in that place.

—John 5:13

The thief does not come, except to steal and kill and destroy. I came that they may have life, and that they may have it more abundantly.

—John 10:10

He has blinded their eyes and hardened their hearts, lest they should see with their eyes and perceive with their hearts and turn, and I would heal them.

—John 12:40

Acts

Then Peter said, Silver and gold have I none; but such as I have give I thee: In the name of Jesus Christ of Nazareth rise up and walk. And he took him by the right hand, and lifted him up: and immediately his feet and ankle bones received strength. And he leaping up stood, and walked, and entered with them into the temple, walking, and leaping, and praising God. And all the people saw him walking and praising God.

—Acts 3:6–9, kjv

As the lame man who was healed held on to Peter and John, all the people ran together to them in the entrance that is called Solomon's Porch, greatly amazed.

—Acts 3:11

But seeing the man who was healed standing with them, they had nothing to say against it.

—Acts 4:14

For the man on whom this miracle of healing was performed was over forty years old.

—Acts 4:22

...by stretching out Your hand to heal and that signs and wonders may be performed in the name of Your holy Son Jesus.

—Acts 4:30

...so that they even brought the sick out into the streets and placed them on beds and mats, that at least the shadow of Peter passing by might touch some of them. Crowds also came out of the cities surrounding Jerusalem, bringing the sick and those who were afflicted by evil spirits, and they were all healed.

—Acts 5:15–16

For unclean spirits, crying with a loud voice, came out of many who were possessed. And many who were paralyzed or lame were healed.

—Acts 8:7

As Peter passed through every region, he came down also to the saints who lived in Lydda. There he found a man named Aeneas, who had been bed-ridden for eight years and was paralyzed. Peter said to him, "Aeneas, Jesus the Christ heals you. Rise up and make your bed." And immediately he rose up.

—Acts 9:32–34

In Joppa there was a disciple named Tabitha, which is translated Dorcas. This woman was full of good works and almsgiving. In those days she became ill and died. And when they had washed her, they placed her in an upper room. Since Lydda was near Joppa, the disciples, hearing that Peter was there, sent two men to him, pleading, "Do not delay to come to us."

Peter rose up and went with them. When he arrived, they led him into the upper room. All the widows stood by him weeping, and showing the tunics and garments which Dorcas had made while she was with them. Peter put them all outside and knelt down and prayed. And turning to the body he said, "Tabitha, arise."

She opened her eyes, and when she saw Peter she sat up.

—Acts 9:36–40

…how God anointed Jesus of Nazareth with the Holy Spirit and with power, who went about doing good and healing all who were oppressed by the devil, for God was with Him.

—Acts 10:38

He heard Paul speaking, who looked intently at him and perceived that he had faith to be healed.

—Acts 14:9

God worked powerful miracles by the hands of Paul. So handkerchiefs or aprons he had touched were brought to the sick, and the diseases left them, and the evil spirits went out of them.

—Acts 19:11–12

So I urge you to eat. This is for your preservation, for not a hair shall fall from your head.

—ACTS 27:34

In that area was an estate of the chief man of the island, named Publius, who had welcomed us and courteously housed us for three days. It happened that the father of Publius lay sick with a fever and dysentery. Paul visited him and, placing his hands on him, prayed and healed him. When this happened, the rest on the island who had diseases also came and were healed.

—ACTS 28:7–9

...for the heart of this people has grown dull. Their ears are hard of hearing, and they have closed their eyes, lest they should see with their eyes and hear with their ears and understand with their heart and turn, and I would heal them.

—ACTS 28:27

Romans

For with the heart one believes unto righteousness, and with the mouth confession is made unto salvation.

—ROMANS 10:10

For by heart me believeth to rightwiseness [Forsooth by heart men believeth to rightwiseness], but by mouth acknowledging is made to health.

—ROMANS 10:10, WYC

For the gifts and calling of God are irrevocable. For just as you once were disobedient to God, but have now received mercy through their disobedience, so these also have now been disobedient, that they also may receive mercy by the mercy shown to you.

—Romans 11:29–31

1 Corinthians

…to another faith by the same Spirit, to another gifts of healings by the same Spirit.

—1 Corinthians 12:9

God has put these in the church: first apostles, second prophets, third teachers, after that miracles, then gifts of healings, helps, governments, and various tongues.

—1 Corinthians 12:28

Do all have the gifts of healings? Do all speak with tongues? Do all interpret?

—1 Corinthians 12:30

Galatians

Christ has redeemed us from the curse of the law by being made a curse for us—as it is written, "Cursed is everyone who hangs on a tree."

—Galatians 3:13

Philippians

Indeed he was sick, near death. But God had mercy on him, and not only on him, but also on me, lest I should have had sorrow upon sorrow.

—PHILIPPIANS 2:27

Hebrews

And make straight paths for your feet, lest that which is lame be turned out of the way; but let it rather be healed.

—HEBREWS 12:13, KJV

James

Is any among you afflicted? let him pray. Is any merry? let him sing psalms. Is any sick among you? let him call for the elders of the church; and let them pray over him, anointing him with oil in the name of the Lord: And the prayer of faith shall save the sick, and the Lord shall raise him up; and if he have committed sins, they shall be forgiven him. Confess your faults one to another, and pray one for another, that ye may be healed. The effectual fervent prayer of a righteous man availeth much.

—JAMES 5:13–16, KJV

1 Peter

Who his own self bare our sins in his own body on the tree, that we, being dead to sins, should live unto righteousness: by whose stripes ye were healed.

—1 PETER 2:24, KJV

1 John

If any man see his brother sin a sin which is not unto death, he shall ask, and he shall give him life for them that sin not unto death. There is a sin unto death: I do not say that he shall pray for it.

—1 JOHN 5:16, KJV

3 John

Beloved, I wish above all things that thou mayest prosper and be in health, even as thy soul prospereth.

—3 JOHN 2, KJV

Revelation

And God shall wipe away all tears from their eyes; and there shall be no more death, neither sorrow, nor crying, neither shall there be any more pain: for the former things are passed away.

—REVELATION 21:4, KJV

In the midst of the street of it, and on either side of the river, was there the tree of life, which bare twelve manner of fruits, and yielded her fruit every month: and the leaves of the tree were for the healing of the nations.

—Revelation 22:2, kjv

Appendix

QUICK REFERENCE GUIDE TO FASTING AND PRAYING FOR HEALING AND DELIVERANCE

UNBELIEF HINDERS US from dealing with strongholds. It takes faith to dislodge the enemy. Fasting helps you overcome unbelief and build strong faith. Fasting with prayer is the supernatural combination that Jesus gave His disciples in Matthew 17. I am not saying that when you fast, you will earn brownie points with God or that you are working your way to enjoying God's blessings. We don't fast to be saved, please God, or go to heaven. There is no law that says if you don't fast, you will go to hell. We fast for breakthrough and revival, for family and loved ones. For the weapons of our warfare are not carnal but mighty through God!

Some things take fasting and prayer. There is no other way around. There are those kinds of demons that just don't give up. They are strong, proud, arrogant, and defiant. They are familiar spirits that have been in your family. But you have to get to the point where you don't care how messed up your family is; you say: "It is stopping with me. This is not going on to another generation. This is it, devil. If my grandmother or grandfather didn't stand against it, if my mother and father didn't defeat it, I'm going to defeat it. I refuse to be poor, broke, sick, rejected, messed up.... No!"

Sometimes you have to do something unusual, extraordinary, and beyond the norm to see breakthrough. Normal church, normal Christianity, normal preaching, and normal praying are not going to get the job done. Some little sweet prayer is not going to do. Religion won't get it done. It is going to take an anointing that destroys the yoke. When you fast, the anointing increases in your life because you are so into the Spirit. The authority of God, power of God, and faith of God come alive when you lay aside some things and fast. You will find yourself getting stronger and stronger. Shouting doesn't do it. It is the anointing that does it.

Isaiah 58 talks about how we can fast to break every yoke to undo the heavy burdens. Fasting makes room so the oppressed go free. Fasting breaks bondages and causes revival.

When you are dealing with a serious issue—maybe you are dealing with something you don't know how to handle—the best thing to do sometimes is to let go of some food for a little while. Pray against that thing. Man may not be able to help you, and you may not know how to defeat it, but with God all things are possible.

As you fast and humble yourself, the grace of God will come upon your life. The Lord will be the strength of your life. What you could not do in the flesh you can do by the Spirit of God—because it's not by might or by power but by the Spirit of the Lord that every mountain is removed!

Listen, extraordinary situations require extraordinary measures. Sometimes it only happens when you get desperate—when you are so tired of being defeated and hindered in an area.

How to Fast

Fasting is beneficial whether you fast partially or fully. One-day fasts on a consistent basis will strengthen your spirit over time and give you the ability to discipline yourself for longer fasts. Three-day fasts with just water are a powerful way to see breakthroughs. Esther and the people of Israel went into a three-day fast when they were seeking deliverance from death at the hand of Haman, the king's evil advisor (Esther 4:16). Fasts longer than three days should be done by people with more experience in fasting.

I do not recommend long fasts unless there is an emergency or if one is led by the Holy Spirit to do so. Daniel fasted twenty-one days and saw a great breakthrough for his people (Dan. 9–10). Daniel was also a prophet, and God will use prophets to fast for different reasons to see breakthroughs. Jesus fasted forty days before beginning

His ministry (Matt. 4:1–2). Moses and Elijah also fasted forty days (Exod. 34:28; Deut. 9:9, 18; 1 Kings 19:8). I do know of people who have fasted forty days and have seen great breakthroughs.

A partial fast can include some food such as vegetables and can be done for long lengths. Complete fasts consist of only water, and water is important to cleanse the system of toxins that are released through fasting. The Holy Spirit will reveal to you when you need to fast. A fasted lifestyle is a powerful lifestyle.

Approach Fasting With Humility and Sincerity

In Jesus's day the Pharisees fasted with attitudes of pride and superiority:

> The Pharisee stood and prayed thus with himself, God, I thank thee, that I am not as other men are....I fast twice in the week.
>
> —LUKE 18:11–12, KJV

Anytime you are full of pride, being legalistic and religious, you can fast and pray all you want, but you won't see many miracles. The Pharisees didn't have any miracles come as a result of their prayer and fasting. They had no power. Jesus had all the miracles because He was humble and full of mercy, love, and compassion toward people. The Pharisees had nothing but long robes on—robes with no miracles. They couldn't heal a headache, a mosquito bite, or a hangnail. They had no power because they were not humble and showed no mercy. Jesus showed up and broke all their rules. He healed the sick, raised the dead, and cast out devils. Then they wanted to kill him. They were not concerned about people. They were more concerned about their position and their title.

Don't ever get to a place where your position or title takes the humility and the mercy of God out of your life. Always be humble. Always be merciful. We must approach fasting with humility. Fasting must be genuine and not religious or hypocritical. This is what God requires in fasting. We must have correct motives in fasting.

Fasting is a powerful tool if done correctly. Muslims and Hindus fast, but their fasts are merely religious. Great miracles and breakthroughs happen when fasting is done in the right spirit. Isaiah chapter 58 describes the fast that God has chosen:

- Fasting cannot be done with amusement (v. 3).

- Fasting cannot be done while mistreating others (v. 3).

- Fasting cannot be done for strife or contention (v. 4).

- Fasting should cause one to bow his head in humility, like a bulrush (v. 5).

- Fasting should be a time of searching the heart and repenting (v. 5).

- Fasting should be done with an attitude of compassion for the lost and hurting (v. 7).

This is the fast that God promises to bless. The enemy knows the power of prayer and fasting, and he will do everything in his power to stop you. Believers who begin to fast can expect to encounter much spiritual resistance. A believer must be committed to a fasted lifestyle. The rewards of fasting far outweigh the obstacles of the enemy.

Prayers to Build Strong Faith

I will forsake any bondage that seeks to entrap me, looking forward by faith and setting my eyes on Him who is invisible (Heb. 11:27).

I decree and declare that by faith I will walk through my trials on dry ground, and my enemies will be drowned (Heb. 11:29).

I will encircle the immovable walls in my life, and by my faith those walls will fall down (Heb. 11:30).

I will subdue kingdoms, rain down righteousness, obtain promises, and stop the mouths of lions because of my faith (Heb. 11:33).

I am established and anointed by God (2 Cor. 1:21).

I activate my mustard seed of faith and say to this mountain of sickness and disease in my life, "Be removed and go to another place." Nothing will be impossible to me (Matt. 17:20).

I declare that I have uncommon, great faith in the power of Jesus Christ, faith that cannot be found anywhere else (Matt. 8:10).

I pray as Your anointed disciples prayed, "Increase my faith!" (Luke 17:5).

I will not stagger at the promise of God through unbelief, but I will stand strong in the faith, giving glory to God (Rom. 4:20).

My faith increases the more I hear, and hear by the Word of God (Rom. 10:17).

I walk by faith and not by sight (2 Cor. 5:7).

I declare that I feel the substance and see the evidence of the things that I have faith for (Heb. 11:1).

I see through the eyes of faith the promise of things afar off. I am persuaded of their reality. I embrace them, knowing that I am a stranger and pilgrim on this earth (Heb. 11:13).

I will stand firm and not waver. I will come boldly before God, asking in faith (James 1:6).

I will not suffer shipwreck in my life, because I have faith and a good conscience (1 Tim. 1:19).

I declare that my faith works together with my works, and by my works my faith is made perfect (James 2:22).

I will show my faith by the works I do (James 2:18).

Because of my faith in Jesus I have boldness and confident access to approach God (Eph. 3:12).

I am a son of Abraham because I have faith (Gal. 3:7).

I am a son of God because I have faith in Christ Jesus (Gal. 3:26).

I go in peace because my faith has saved me (Luke 7:50).

My faith is alive (James 2:17).

The Spirit of God has given me the gift of faith (1 Cor. 12:9).

I have faith in God (Mark 11:22).

Let it be to me according to my faith (Matt. 9:29).

No man has dominion over my faith. I stand by faith (2 Cor. 1:24).

Like Stephen, I do great wonders and signs because I am full of faith (Acts 6:8).

My faith is not in the wisdom of men but in the power of God (1 Cor. 2:5).

I will not be sluggish. I will imitate those who through faith and patience inherit the promises of God (Heb. 6:12).

The just shall live by faith (Rom. 1:17).

The righteousness of God is revealed to me through faith in Jesus (Rom. 3:22).

I am justified by my faith in Jesus (Rom. 3:26).

I have access by faith to the grace of God (Rom. 5:2).

I am raised to life through faith in Christ (Col. 2:12).

By faith I receive the promise of God in my life (Gal. 3:22).

My faith and hope are in God (1 Pet. 1:21).

My faith will not fail (Luke 22:32).

By faith the promise of God is sure to me, the seed of Abraham (Rom. 4:16).

I pray the prayer of faith and will see the sick saved and raised up (James 5:15).

I take the shield of faith and quench all the fiery darts of the wicked one (Eph. 6:16).

I put on the breastplate of faith and love (1 Thess. 5:8).

I obtain for myself good standing and great boldness in my faith in Christ Jesus (1 Tim. 3:13).

Prayers to Release Healing

I will live and not die, and I will proclaim the name of the Lord (Ps. 118:17).

Lord, You heal all my diseases (Ps. 103:3).

Heal me, O Lord, and I will be healed (Jer. 17:14).

Jesus, arise over my life with healing in Your wings (Mal. 4:2).

I prosper and walk in health even as my soul prospers (3 John 2).

I am healed by the stripes of Jesus (Isa. 53:5).

Jesus carried my sickness and infirmities (Matt. 8:17).

I cast out all spirits of infirmity that would attack my body in the name of Jesus.

I break, rebuke, and cast out any spirit of cancer that would attempt to establish itself in my lungs, bones, breast, throat, back, spine, liver, kidneys, pancreas, skin, or stomach in the name of Jesus.

I rebuke and cast out all spirits causing diabetes, high blood pressure, low blood pressure, heart attack, stroke, kidney failure, leukemia, blood disease, breathing problems, arthritis, lupus, Alzheimer's, or insomnia in the name of Jesus.

I speak healing and strength to my bones, muscles, joints, organs, head, eyes, throat, glands, blood, marrow, lungs, kidneys, liver, spleen, spine, pancreas, eyes, bladder, ears, nose, sinuses, mouth, tongue, and feet in the name of Jesus.

I loose myself from all heart attacks rooted in fear, and I command all spirits of fear to leave in Jesus's name (Luke 21:26).

I loose myself from all cancer rooted in bitterness, unforgiveness, resentment, and slander of the tongue, and I command these spirits to come out in the name of Jesus.

I loose myself from lupus rooted in self-rejection, self-hatred, and guilt, and I cast these spirits out in the name of Jesus.

I loose myself from all multiple sclerosis rooted in self-hatred, guilt, and rejection from the father, and I cast these spirits out in the name of Jesus.

I loose myself from rheumatoid arthritis that is rooted in self-hatred and low self-esteem, and I command these spirits to come out in the name of Jesus.

I loose myself from high cholesterol that is rooted in anger and hostility and command these spirits to come out in the name of Jesus.

I loose myself from all sinus problems rooted in fear and anxiety, and I command these spirits to come out in the name of Jesus.

I loose myself from all high blood pressure rooted in fear and anxiety, and I command these spirits to come out in the name of Jesus.

I loose myself from asthma rooted in fear concerning relationships in the name of Jesus.

I loose myself from a weakened immune system that is rooted in a broken spirit or broken heart, and I command these spirits to come out in the name of Jesus.

I loose myself from all strokes rooted in self-rejection, self-bitterness, and self-hatred, and I command these spirits to come out in the name of Jesus.

I loose myself from all bone diseases rooted in envy and jealousy, and I command these spirits to come out in the name of Jesus (Prov. 14:30).

Forgive me, Lord, for allowing any fear, guilt, self-rejection, self-hatred, unforgiveness, bitterness, sin, pride, or rebellion to open the door to any sickness or infirmity. I renounce these things in the name of Jesus.

Prayers for General Deliverance

Keep my soul, and deliver me (Ps. 25:20).

Be pleased, O Lord, to deliver me (Ps. 40:13).

Make haste, O God, and deliver me (Ps. 70:1).

Deliver me in Your righteousness (Ps. 71:2).

Deliver me, O God, out of the hand of the enemy (Ps. 71:4).

Deliver me from my persecutors (Ps. 142:6).

Deliver me out of great waters (Ps. 144:7).

Deliver me from the oppression of man (Ps. 119:134).

Deliver me according to Your Word (Ps. 119:170).

Deliver my soul from lying lips and a deceitful tongue (Ps. 120:2).

Deliver me from my enemies and hide me (Ps. 143:9).

Surround me with songs of deliverance (Ps. 32:7).

Command deliverances for my life (Ps. 44:4).

Deliver me from all my fears (Ps. 34:4).

Deliver me out of all my trouble (Ps. 54:7).

Deliver me from them who hate me (Ps. 69:14).

Deliver me out of my distresses (Ps. 107:6).

Send Your Word and deliver me out of destruction (Ps. 107:20).

Deliver my soul from death, my eyes from tears, and my feet from falling (Ps. 116:8).

I call upon the name of Jesus, and I am delivered (Joel 2:32).

Deliver me from the power of the lion (Dan. 6:27).

Through Your knowledge I am delivered (Prov. 11:9).

Through Your wisdom I am delivered (Prov. 28:26).

I receive miracles of deliverance for my life (Dan. 6:27).

Prayers for Deliverance From Evil

Deliver me from evil (Matt. 6:13).

I pray that You would keep me from evil (1 Chron. 4:10).

No evil will touch me (Job 5:19).

Put to shame those who wish me evil (Ps. 40:14).

Let no evil disease cleave to my body (Ps. 41:8).

I will not be afraid of evil tidings (Ps. 112:7).

I will not be visited with evil (Prov. 19:23).

I refrain my feet from every evil way so that I might keep Your Word (Ps. 119:101).

Preserve me from all evil (Ps. 121:7).

Deliver me from the evil man (Ps. 140:1).

Let people be healed of plagues and evil spirits (Luke 7:21).

I pray that You would keep me from evil (John 17:15).

Let evil spirits be cast out (Acts 19:12).

I will not be overcome with evil, but I overcome evil with good (Rom. 12:21).

I put on the whole armor of God, that I might stand in the evil day (Eph. 6:13).

I cancel all the plans and forces of evil sent against my life.

Let the works of evil be burned by Your holy fire.

Let men repent of evil and turn to righteousness.

Let no evil be established in my life, but let Your righteousness be established.

I loose myself from all evildoers and evil soul ties.

Prayers for Self-Deliverance

I break all generational curses of pride, rebellion, lust, poverty, witchcraft, idolatry, death, destruction, failure, sickness, infirmity, fear, schizophrenia, and rejection in the name of Jesus.

I command all generational and hereditary spirits operating in my life through curses to be bound and cast out in the name of Jesus.

I command all spirits of lust, perversion, adultery, fornication, uncleanness, and immorality to come out of my sexual character in the name of Jesus.

I command all spirits of hurt, rejection, fear, anger, wrath, sadness, depression, discouragement, grief, bitterness, and unforgiveness to come out of my emotions in the name of Jesus.

I command all spirits of confusion, forgetfulness, mind control, mental illness, double-mindedness, fantasy, pain, pride, and memory recall to come out of my mind in the name of Jesus.

I break all curses of schizophrenia and command all spirits of double-mindedness, rejection, rebellion, and root of bitterness to come out in the name of Jesus.

I command all spirits of guilt, shame, and condemnation to come out of my conscience in the name of Jesus.

I command all spirits of pride, stubbornness, disobedience, rebellion, self-will, selfishness, and arrogance to come out of my will in the name of Jesus.

I command all spirits of addiction to come out of my appetite in the name of Jesus.

I command all spirits of witchcraft, sorcery, divination, and occult to come out in the name of Jesus.

I command all spirits operating in my head, eyes, mouth, tongue, and throat to come out in the name of Jesus.

I command all spirits operating in my chest and lungs to come out in the name of Jesus.

I command all spirits operating in my back and spine to come out in the name of Jesus.

I command all spirits operating in my stomach, navel, and abdomen to come out in the name of Jesus.

I command all spirits operating in my heart, spleen, kidneys, liver, and pancreas to come out in the name of Jesus.

I command all spirits operating in my sexual organs to come out in the name of Jesus.

I command all spirits operating in my hands, arms, legs, and feet to come out in the name of Jesus.

I command all demons operating in my skeletal system, including my bones, joints, knees, and elbows, to come out in the name of Jesus.

I command all spirits operating in my glands and endocrine system to come out in the name of Jesus.

I command all spirits operating in my blood and circulatory systems to come out in the name of Jesus.

I command all spirits operating in my muscles and muscular system to come out in the name of Jesus.

I command all religious spirits of doubt, unbelief, error, heresy, and tradition that came in through religion to come out in the name of Jesus.

I command all spirits from my past that are hindering my present and future to come out in the name of Jesus.

I command all ancestral spirits that entered through my ancestors to come out in the name of Jesus.

I command all hidden spirits hiding in any part of my life to come out in the name of Jesus.

RESOURCES

HEALING AND DELIVERANCE are topics that are central to my ministry. I have preached and written on both topics extensively. Here is a list of books and resources for further reading and research.

- *Deliverance and Spiritual Warfare Manual*
- *Destroying the Spirit of Rejection*
- *Fasting for Breakthrough and Deliverance*
- *God's Covenant With You for Deliverance and Freedom*
- *Prayers That Rout Demons*
- *Prayers That Break Curses*
- *Prayers That Bring Healing Unshakeable*

For MP3s and other recordings of my messages on these topics, visit my website at www.johneckhardt.global.

NOTES

CHAPTER 2
FAITH IN THE OLD TESTAMENT

1. Blue Letter Bible, s.v. "aman," accessed June 7, 2017, https://www.blueletterbible.org/lang/lexicon/lexicon.cfm?Strongs=H539&t=KJV.

2. Ibid., s.v. "amen," accessed June 7, 2017, https://www.blueletterbible.org/lang/lexicon/lexicon.cfm?Strongs=H539&t=KJV.

3. Basic Training Bible Ministries, accessed June 7, 2017, http://www.basictraining.org/print.php?nid=205.

4. Blue Letter Bible, s.v. "qavah," accessed June 7, 2017, https://www.blueletterbible.org/lang/lexicon/lexicon.cfm?t=kjv&strongs=h6960.

5. Ibid.

CHAPTER 3
FAITH IN THE NEW TESTAMENT

1. Blue Letter Bible, s.v. "pistis," accessed June 7, 2017, https://www.blueletterbible.org/lang/lexicon/lexicon.cfm?Strongs=G4102&t=KJV.

Chapter 4
Deliverance Is a Gift From God

1. Blue Letter Bible, s.v. "ecar," accessed June 7, 2017, https://www.blueletterbible.org/lang/lexicon/lexicon.cfm?Strongs=H632&t=KJV.

2. Ibid., s.v. "deo," accessed June 7, 2017, https://www.blueletterbible.org/lang/lexicon/lexicon.cfm?Strongs=G1210&t=KJV.

3. Ibid., s.v. "desmeuo," accessed June 7, 2017, https://www.blueletterbible.org/lang/lexicon/lexicon.cfm?Strongs=G1195&t=KJV.

4. Ibid., s.v. "desmeo," accessed June 7, 2017, https://www.blueletterbible.org/lang/lexicon/lexicon.cfm?Strongs=G1196&t=KJV.

5. Ibid., s.v. "garash," accessed June 7, 2017, https://www.blueletterbible.org/lang/lexicon/lexicon.cfm?Strongs=H1644&t=KJV.

6. Ibid., s.v. "ekballo," accessed June 7, 2017, https://www.blueletterbible.org/lang/lexicon/lexicon.cfm?Strongs=G1544&t=KJV.

7. Ibid., s.v. "natsal," accessed June 7, 2017, https://www.blueletterbible.org/lang/lexicon/lexicon.cfm?Strongs=H5337&t=KJV.

8. Ibid., s.v. "chalats," accessed June 7, 2017, https://www.blueletterbible.org/lang/lexicon/lexicon.cfm?Strongs=H2502&t=KJV.

9. Ibid., s.v. "rhyomai," accessed June 7, 2017, https://www.blueletterbible.org/lang/lexicon/lexicon.cfm?Strongs=G4506&t=KJV.

10. Ibid., s.v. "palat," accessed June 7, 2017, https://www.blueletterbible.org/lang/lexicon/lexicon.cfm?Strongs=H6403&t=KJV.

11. Ibid., s.v. "lytrotes," accessed June 7, 2017, https://www.blueletterbible.org/lang/lexicon/lexicon.cfm?Strongs=G3086&t=KJV.

12. Ibid., s.v. "rhyomai," accessed June 7, 2017, https://www.blueletterbible.org/lang/lexicon/lexicon.cfm?t=kjv&strongs=g4506.

13. Ibid., s.v. "daimoniodes," accessed June 7, 2017, https://www.blueletterbible.org/lang/lexicon/lexicon.cfm?Strongs=G1141&t=KJV.

14. Ibid., s.v. "radah," accessed June 7, 2017, https://www.blueletterbible.org/lang/lexicon/lexicon.cfm?Strongs=H7287&t=KJV.

15. Ibid., s.v. "mashal," accessed June 7, 2017, https://www.blueletterbible.org/lang/lexicon/lexicon.cfm?Strongs=H4910&t=KJV.

16. Ibid., s.v. "kyrieuo," accessed June 7, 2017, https://www.blueletterbible.org/lang/lexicon/lexicon.cfm?Strongs=G2961&t=KJV.

17. Ibid., s.v. "pethach," accessed June 7, 2017, https://www.blueletterbible.org/lang/lexicon/lexicon.cfm?Strongs=H6607&t=KJV.

18. Ibid., s.v. "thyra," accessed June 7, 2017, https://www.blueletterbible.org/lang/lexicon/lexicon.cfm?Strongs=G2374&t=KJV.

19. Ibid., s.v. "derowr," accessed June 7, 2017, https://www.blueletterbible.org/lang/lexicon/lexicon.cfm?Strongs=H1865&t=KJV.

20. Ibid., s.v. "aphesis," accessed June 7, 2017, https://www.blueletterbible.org/lang/lexicon/lexicon.cfm?Strongs=G859&t=KJV.

21. Ibid., s.v. "pathach," accessed June 7, 2017, https://www.blueletterbible.org/lang/lexicon/lexicon.cfm?Strongs=H6605&t=KJV.

22. Ibid., s.v. "lyo," accessed June 7, 2017, https://www.blueletterbible.org/lang/lexicon/lexicon.cfm?Strongs=G3089&t=KJV.

23. Ibid., s.v. "ashaq," accessed June 7, 2017, https://www.blueletterbible.org/lang/lexicon/lexicon.cfm?Strongs=H6231&t=KJV.

24. Ibid., s.v. "katadynasteuo," accessed June 7, 2017, https://www.blueletterbible.org/lang/lexicon/lexicon.cfm?Strongs=G2616&t=KJV.

25. Ibid., s.v. "daimonizomai," accessed June 7, 2017, https://www.blueletterbible.org/lang/lexicon/lexicon.cfm?Strongs=G1139&t=KJV.

26. Ibid., s.v. "satan," accessed June 7, 2017, https://www.blueletterbible.org/lang/lexicon/lexicon.cfm?Strongs=H7854&t=KJV.

27. Ibid., s.v. "diabolos," accessed June 7, 2017, https://www.blueletterbible.org/lang/lexicon/lexicon.cfm?Strongs=G1228&t=KJV.

28. Ibid., s.v. "yasha," accessed June 7, 2017, https://www.blueletterbible.org/lang/lexicon/lexicon.cfm?Strongs=H3467&t=KJV.

29. Ibid., s.v. "sozo," accessed June 7, 2017, https://www.blueletterbible.org/lang/lexicon/lexicon.cfm?Strongs=G4982&t=KJV.

30. Ibid., s.v. "ra'a," accessed June 7, 2017, https://www.blueletterbible.org/lang/lexicon/lexicon.cfm?Strongs=H7489&t=KJV.

31. Ibid., s.v. "dachaq," accessed June 7, 2017, https://www.blueletterbible.org/lang/lexicon/lexicon.cfm?Strongs=H1766&t=KJV.

32. Ibid., s.v. "ochleo," accessed June 7, 2017, https://www.blueletterbible.org/lang/lexicon/lexicon.cfm?Strongs=G3791&t=KJV.

33. Ibid., s.v. "kataponeo," accessed June 7, 2017, https://www.blueletterbible.org/lang/lexicon/lexicon.cfm?Strongs=G2669&t=KJV.

Chapter 7
By His Stripes You Are Healed

1. Blue Letter Bible, s.v. "rapha," accessed June 7, 2017, https://www.blueletterbible.org/lang/lexicon/lexicon.cfm?Strongs=H7495&t=KJV.

2. Ibid., s.v. "marpe," accessed June 7, 2017, https://www.blueletterbible.org/lang/lexicon/lexicon.cfm?Strongs=H4832&t=KJV.

3. Ibid., s.v. "aruwkah," accessed June 7, 2017, https://www.blueletterbible.org/lang/lexicon/lexicon.cfm?Strongs=H724&t=KJV.

4. Ibid., s.v. "therapeuo," accessed June 7, 2017, https://www.blueletterbible.org/lang/lexicon/lexicon.cfm?Strongs=G2323&t=KJV.

5. Ibid., s.v. "diasozo," accessed June 7, 2017, https://www.blueletterbible.org/lang/lexicon/lexicon.cfm?Strongs=G1295&t=KJV.

6. Ibid.

7. Ibid., s.v. "choliy," accessed June 7, 2017, https://www.blueletterbible.org/lang/lexicon/lexicon.cfm?Strongs=H2483&t=KJV.

Chapter 8
Healing in the Old Testament

1. The Voice of Healing, "Healing in the Old Testament," VoiceofHealing.info, accessed June 7, 2017, http://www.voiceofhealing.info/02history/oldtestament.html.

CONNECT WITH US!

(Spiritual Growth)

Facebook.com/CharismaHouse

@CharismaHouse

Instagram.com/CharismaHouse

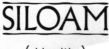

(Health)

Pinterest.com/CharismaHouse

(Bible)
www.mevbible.com